W9-BRG-821

HOCKEY

Learn to Play the Modern Way

Sports Illustrated Winner's Circle Books

BOOKS ON TEAM SPORTS

Baseball
Basketball
Football: Winning Defense
Football: Winning Offense
Hockey
Lacrosse
Pitching
Soccer
Volleyball

BOOKS ON INDIVIDUAL SPORTS

Bowling
Competitive Swimming
Cross-Country Skiing
Figure Skating
Golf
Putting
Racquetballl
Running for Women
Skiing
Squash
Tennis
Track: Championship Running
Track: The Field Events

SPECIAL BOOKS

Backpacking
Canoeing
Fly Fishing
Scuba Diving
Small-Boat Sailing
Strength Training
Training with Weights

Sports Illustrated
HOCKEY
Learn to Play the Modern Way

by Jack Falla

Photography by Heinz Kluetmeier

Sports Illustrated
Winner's Circle Books

To everyone who has skated
in my backyard rink,
The Bacon Street Omni

The author would like to thank Babson College, Wellesley, Massachusetts; the Babson Athletic Department; and former Babson hockey players James Gavin, Steve Thomas and Steve Villa for their help with the photography for this book. Besides being technically competent and thoroughly cooperative, the players added new meaning to the expression "the old college try," that is, those body checking photographs are not "staged." Finally, thanks to referee Jim Cerbo who appears in these pages courtesy of the Eastern College Athletic Conference.

Photo credits: For *Sports Illustrated:* Paul Bereswell: pp. 3, 15, 82, 87, 105, 124, 156; Bill Jaspersohn: pp. 25, 27 (bottom); Richard Mackson: p. 52; Tony Tomsic: p. 70; Tony Triolo: pp. 83, 88; Manny Millan: p. 154; George Tiedemann: pp. 122, 186; Jerry Wachter: pp. 172, 184; David E. Klutho: pp. 32, 39, 122, 183, 192, 194; Brian Lanker: pp. 196, 201; Bob Sacha: pp. 212, 218. All other photographs by Heinz Kluetmeier. Project editor: Bill Jaspersohn.

Copyright © 1987, 1994 by Time Inc.

All rights reserved. No part of this book may be reproduced in any form or by any electronic or mechanical means, including information storage and retrieval systems, without written permission from the publisher, except by a reviewer who may quote passage in a review.

FIRST SPORTS ILLUSTRATED BOOKS EDITION 1994
Sports Illustrated Hockey: Learn to Play the Modern Way was originally published by Time, Inc. in 1987.

Sports Illustrated Books
An imprint of Madison Books, Inc.
Lanham, MD 20706

Distributed by National Book Network

Library of Congress Cataloging in Publication Data

Falla, Jack, 1944–
Sports illustrated hockey : learn to play the modern way / by Jack Falla ; photography by Heinz Kluetmeier. — 1st Sports Illustrated Books ed.
p. cm.
Previously published: New York : Sports Illustrated, © 1987.
1. Hockey. I. Kluetmeier, Heinz. II. Sports illustrated (Time, inc.) III. Title.
IV. Title: Hockey.
[GV847.F18 1993] 796.962—dc20 93–28165 CIP

ISBN 1–56800–004–9 (paperback : alk. paper)

Contents

Introduction

Why a new hockey book?

Mainly because in recent years hockey has become a new game. The hockey of today and, presumably, of the foreseeable future, is a faster, more intricate and more sophisticated game than the hockey of any previous decade.

For most of this century, North American hockey was characterized by simple, linear patterns of play, sharply defined player roles and an emphasis on individual skill over team tactics. Right and left wings stayed on their respective sides of the ice, centers generally stayed in the middle lane, defensemen rarely played a major role in a team's attack and goalies merely stood in front of the net waiting for an opponent to take a shot.

In its recent and fairly sudden evolutionary leap, today's game is characterized by creative, weaving offenses; flexible, attack-triggering defenses; hybrid power plays and penalty-killing systems; and by a new breed of mobile goaltender as adept at stickhandling and passing the puck as he is at stopping it. Several forces have brought about these changes. In 1972 there was the highly publicized 8-game series between a team of National Hockey League stars and the Soviet National Team. Though the NHL narrowly won the series 4-3-1 on Paul Henderson's goal in the closing minutes of the final game, the Soviets demonstrated the value of superb physical conditioning (particularly upper-body and arm strength), creative use of neutral ice, and precision on the power play—all elements that would begin to work their way into the North American game. Later in the 1970s and continuing into the '80s, a rising tide of European players, particularly Swedes, began to show up in the North American professional ranks, bringing with them great individual puckhandling, and passing and skating skills, abilities that helped "open up" North American skate-and-shoot offenses.

Then, in 1980, a brilliant coach from the University of Minnesota, Herb

9

The victorious 1980 U.S. Men's Olympic Hockey Team
helped bring a new era of hockey to America.

10   Brooks, successfully blended a kind of European offensive creativity with the traditional North American strengths of tough physical play, tenacious defense and outstanding goaltending to produce the famous "Miracle on Ice," the United States' gold medal for hockey at the Winter Olympics in Lake Placid. That victory established the legitimacy of the swirling, weaving patterns of play that some writers, coaches and players were beginning to call "Euro-hockey."

In the 1980s we saw the ascendency of the National Hockey League's Edmonton Oilers who, led by the playmaking and scoring of Wayne Gretzky, won consecutive Stanley Cups in 1984 and 1985 and a third Cup in 1987. By contrast to the defense-oriented, close-checking Stanley Cup championship teams of the past, the Oilers won on the strength of a dazzling high-speed offense, the keys to which were constant puck and player movement.

To me, hockey has changed enough that it's time to expand and update the game's instructional literature.

It's worth noting, though, that hockey's fundamental skills—skating, puck-handling, passing and shooting—have remained essentially unchanged. Thus, while this book contains up-to-the-minute material on team offense, defense and special team systems as well as coaching and training techniques, it also contains chapters for you young players on the game's fundamentals.

Besides tactics and techniques, we'll take a close look at the critical areas of coaching technique, sports psychology, nutrition and off ice training. You'll even find a special appendix devoted solely to the problems that often face the volunteer youth coach: the man or woman whose willingness and good intentions often exceed his or her knowledge. May this "Survival Manual for the Volunteer Coach" help those tens of thousands of coaches who, in working with the 750,000 U.S. and Canadian amateur players, have a major impact on the growth and direction of the game.

Finally, we'll move from the business of instruction, drills and tactics to enter the often-ignored realm of fun. Chapter Ten, "Building a Rink of Your Own," is intended not only for the young player looking for extra practice time, but for anyone who lives in a climate conducive to natural ice and who would like a private place to experience the simple joys of skating or playing pick-up hockey.

This is a *practical* book for players, coaches and those spectators who seek a deeper understanding of a changing game. But no matter what changes hockey has undergone in recent years, it, like all other games, is still shaped and controlled by the people who play, coach and watch it. I hope that this book will contribute to a hockey marked by technical proficiency, tactical creativity, a respect for the spirit of the rules and an enduring sense of fun.

Keys to Diagrams

Below is a listing of the key elements in the diagrams that appear throughout this book.

○ = Offensive player

▪ = Defensive player

⟶ = Path of puck carrier or other play

----▶ = Pass or shot

LW = Left wing

RW = Right wing

D = Defense

LD = Left defense

RD = Right defense

C = Center

G = Goaltender

FC = Forechecker

PC = Puck carrier

P = Pointman

F = Forward

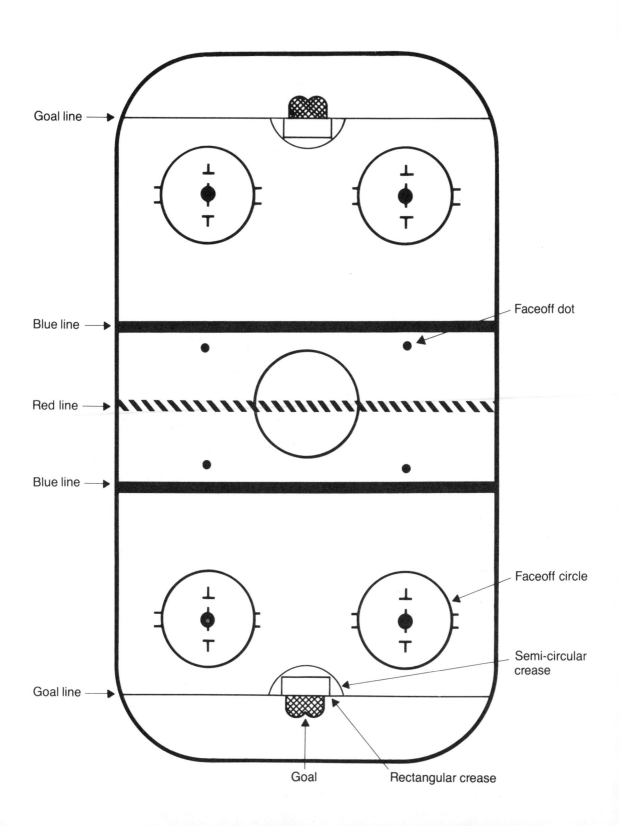

Goal line

Blue line

Red line

Blue line

Goal line

Faceoff dot

Faceoff circle

Semi-circular crease

Goal

Rectangular crease

1

Rink, Rules and Equipment

Hockey may not be an easy game but it is a simple one. It has few complex rules (certainly nothing as initially bewildering as baseball's infield fly rule) and its object is simple: to shoot a 3-inch-wide, 2-inch-thick, 6-ounce, frozen vulcanized rubber disc, called a puck, into a 6-foot-wide, 4-foot-high goal. The team with the most goals wins.

THE RINK

Hockey rinks in North America generally measure 200 × 85 feet with rounded corners. The ice surface is surrounded by boards 3½ to 4 feet high, on top of which is a barrier of shatterproof glass, or, on some older rinks, chain-link fence, to protect spectators from flying pucks and sticks, and to keep the puck in play.

A few rinks—for example, NHL rinks in Boston (191 × 83 ft.), Buffalo (196 × 85 ft.) and Chicago (185 × 85 ft.)—are slightly smaller than regulation size. A smaller ice surface tends to reward tough physical play. There are also larger-than-standard ice surfaces such as the 200 × 90 ft. rink at the U.S. Military Academy, West Point, N.Y. These rinks reward good skating, conditioning and offensive creativity.

European rinks and rinks used in Olympic and World Championship competition are generally 200 × 100 ft. (The Saddledome rink in Calgary, Alberta, Canada, site of the 1988 Winter Olympics, was built with movable boards to permit enlarging it to Olympic size.) It is not surprising that European players, having spent most of their careers on large ice surfaces, are noted for their skating, stickhandling and passing, while many North American players, who have traditionally played on smaller rinks, are noted for their tough, grinding play along the boards and in the corners.

13

Though rinks can vary somewhat in size, they all
contain the components shown here.

GOALS AND ICE SURFACE

The goal posts and net are located 10 feet from the ends of the rink. While goal cages formerly were fastened to the ice on immovable pins, a recent trend has seen rink owners switching to magnetized pins and posts. With the magnetic system, the goalpost will give way if a player collides with it, reducing the risk of serious injury.

A 2-inch wide red line—the goal line—runs between the vertical goal posts, across the rink and up the sides of the boards. A goal is scored only when the puck *completely* crosses this line between the posts and under the crossbar. The rectangular area marked in red in front of the goal—it is a semi-circular area in college, Olympic and international play—is the goaltender's "crease." No opposing player is permitted to enter the crease; if one does and if, at the same time, his team happens to score, the goal is disallowed. The only exception occurs when the referee decides that the player in the crease was pushed or held there by an opponent. Goaltenders and defensemen will battle furiously to protect the crease. Opposing players who venture into or near that goal mouth area often do so at the risk of heavy body checks.

The two 1-foot-wide blue lines drawn 60 feet from the goal lines at each end of the rink divide the ice into offensive, defensive and neutral zones. Like the goal lines, the blue lines extend completely across the rink and up the boards. The area between the blue lines is the "neutral zone" or "center ice." It is bisected by a red line, which, like the blue lines, is 1 foot wide and extends across the ice and up the boards. (If you're wondering how they get these lines on the ice, it's done with either ribbons or paint after the ice is made. The lines are then covered with several thin, protective layers of ice.)

The ice is also marked with five red "faceoff circles," each with a 15-foot radius, located near each of the four corners of the rink and at center ice. Four other faceoff areas are designated by the red dots, two on the neutral ice side of each blue line. In faceoffs—hockey's equivalent to the jump ball in basketball—an official drops the puck between opposing players. Faceoffs occur at center ice at the start of each period and after a goal has been scored. They occur at one of the other designated faceoff spots every time there is a stoppage of play. Most faceoffs in the circles in the defensive zone occur *after* the defending team has managed to stop play, while the four neutral ice faceoff dots are used most often for faceoffs following offsides violations (more on these matters later).

PLAYERS

Each team is permitted to start a game with six players on the ice. They are: a goaltender, two defensemen (left and right) and three forwards (left wing, right wing and center). The goaltender usually plays the entire 60-minute game while, because of the fatiguing level of play, the other players generally stay on the ice for shifts that run between 45 seconds and 2 minutes. Most teams rotate three or four forward lines and two or three pairings of defensemen. Unlike most other sports, hockey allows substitutions "on the fly"—a tricky maneuver and one that, if not done properly, will find a team either defensively vulnerable because it has too few men on the ice or penalized for having an extra skater. (The latter mix-up occurred in the seventh and deciding game of the 1979 Stanley Cup semifinals when Boston, leading Montreal by a goal late in the third period, had an extra forward jump onto the ice during a change on the fly. Montreal scored on the ensuing power play and went on to win the game in overtime en route to its fourth consecutive Stanley Cup.)

Substituting "on the fly" is one of hockey's more unusual—and tricky—features.

A team should change on the fly only when it is moving to the attack, not when the puck is in its defensive zone. Most teams will get the puck over the red line (to avoid having the play called back for "icing"—see below), then shoot or "dump" it into the attacking zone while all five players come off the ice and their replacements come on. If you are sitting near the players' bench you may hear the returning players yelling out their positions—"Center," "Left Wing"—so that players standing by will know who should be coming onto the ice. That minimizes the chance of two players, in their eagerness, jumping out to replace one.

RULES

A hockey game is usually 60 minutes long with play divided into three 20-minute periods, although in some high school and youth hockey leagues the game may be played in periods of 15, 12 or even 10 minutes. Overtime to decide ties is at the discretion of the league. In the NHL, teams play a 5-minute sudden-death overtime after which, if the score is still tied, the result is entered in the record as a tie. Playoffs in almost all leagues are decided by sudden-death overtime: first team to score wins.

Hockey has two important technical rules you must understand to play and appreciate the game, *offside* and *icing*.

Offside

There are two ways a play can be ruled offside:

1. Two-line pass: When a player passes the puck across two lines (blue and red) to a teammate, the play is offside. The referee will whistle the action dead and order a faceoff at the point where the offside pass originated.

2. A play is also offside any time an attacking player precedes the puck across the blue line and into the attacking zone. Here, the ensuing faceoff will be at one of the faceoff dots outside the blue line.

It is important to know that it is your *skates*, not your stick or the puck, that determines an offside violation. You are offside only when *both* skates have crossed the outer edge of the red or blue line. Thus, you can straddle a line—keeping one skate in onside territory—and not be ruled offside.

Offside

Offside occurs either when a player passes the puck across two lines to a teammate (A), or when an attacking player precedes the puck across the blue line and into the attacking zone (B). Result: Play is whistled dead and a face-off occurs.

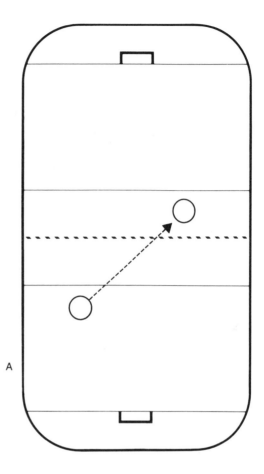

A

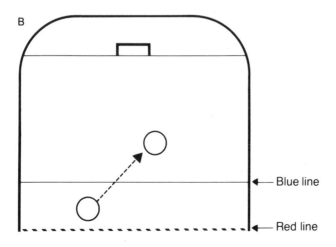

B

← Blue line

← Red line

Icing

Icing occurs when the defending team—usually in a desperate response to heavy offensive pressure—shoots the puck from its half of the ice down to the other end of the rink and across the red goal line, and an opponent other than the goaltender touches the puck first. But icing brings only fleeting relief for the defensive team because, on an icing call, the puck is brought back for a faceoff in the zone of the team that "iced" it. The only time you may ice the puck legally is when your team is playing short-handed, trying to kill a penalty.

A relatively recent innovation in college and amateur hockey is the "automatic icing" rule. Here, the referee whistles the play dead immediately after the puck crosses the goal line rather than waiting until it is touched by a player on the non-offending side. This eliminates the dangerous headlong races between opposing players to get to the puck first. Automatic icing is a particularly sound policy in youth leagues, in which players' skating abilities may not be advanced enough for

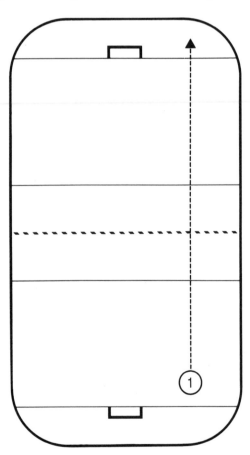

Icing.
Icing occurs when the defending team shoots the puck from its half of the ice all the way past its opponent's red goal line, and an opponent other than the goaltender touches it first. Result: face-off in the icing team's zone.

them to go from full-speed to a quick stop without a high risk of losing their footing and slamming into the boards.

PENALTIES

The speed and the physical nature of the game make penalties an almost inescapable part of hockey. Some penalties, such as tripping, are sometimes accidental. Others, like holding and hooking, are almost always deliberate and usually occur when a defender who has been beaten makes one last, desperate attempt to restrain an opponent. Still other penalties, such as high-sticking, slashing, and spearing, are the inexcusable results of undisciplined tempers. It is these vicious infractions that too often give hockey its reputation as an excessively violent game.

Yet the source of violence in hockey lies in the inclinations of a few players and not in the nature of the game itself, particularly today's game, with its stress on skating and puck skills. Hockey will always be a contact sport. But it need not be a violent sport. Tighter officiating, the instilling of sportsmanship at the youth levels, and stronger sanctions against fighting, high-sticking and spearing at all levels (but, especially, in the trend-setting, image-creating professional leagues) will go a long way toward eliminating the violence that does exist. Hockey's most frequently called penalties are:

Holding: Using your hands to grab either your opponent or his stick.

Penalties

Holding.
Whether you grab an opponent's body (A), or stick (B), you can be whistled off for a minor penalty.

A

B

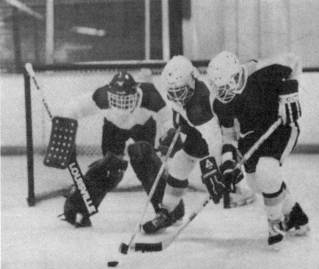

Tripping: Toppling your opponent. Tripping, even more than holding, is usually the last-ditch act of a beaten defender. But tripping is a judgment call, forcing the referee to determine whether a player A) was illegally tripped by the stick, knee, foot, arm, hand or elbow of another player, B) fell down as a result of incidental and legal contact or C) "took a dive," that is, manufactured an exaggerated sprawl over an opponent's stick or leg in hope of drawing a penalty.

Tripping.
Tripping is usually a beaten defender's last-ditch means of stopping the puck carrier. Here, the player on the left will be taking his own trip—to the penalty box.

Hooking.
The player in white is using his stick illegally as a "hook" to restrain the puck carrier.

Hooking: Using the blade of your stick to restrain an opponent.

Interference: Checking an opponent who does not have the puck. Since there is so much contact in hockey, interference is another judgment call. Referees— particularly in college and the pros—tend to be lenient with interference calls against players who are jostling for position in front of the net.

Slashing: Using your stick to hit, or *attempt* to hit, an opposing player. The stick need not make contact if the referee decides there was intent to injure.

Charging: Applying a body check after you have taken more than two deliberate steps toward the victim or jumped against the opponent. When a charge sends the victim crashing into the boards, the penalty may be called for "boarding."

Spearing: Using your stick literally as a spear to stab at an opponent. This is one of the most serious transgressions in hockey and calls for an automatic 5-minute "major" penalty. As in slashing and high-sticking, it is the *intent* to spear, rather than the actual contact, that determines the call.

Spearing.
Spearing is using your stick to stab at an opponent, as the player on the right is doing. Such dangerous and unsportsman-like actions warrant their five-minute penalties.

Elbowing: Delivering a check with your arms or elbows instead of with your body. (Tip: When making a body check, keep your stick down, which will keep your arms down and thus help you avoid calls for elbowing or high-sticking.)

Elbowing.
It's legal to check with your shoulder or hip but not with your elbows.

High-sticking and cross-checking. The player on the right could be penalized for one of two infractions— high sticking (carrying his stick above shoulder level while moving toward an opponent) or cross-checking (hitting an opponent with both hands on the stick and no part of the stick on the ice).

High-sticking: Carrying your stick above shoulder level when moving toward an opponent.

Cross-checking: Hitting your opponent with both hands on your stick and no part of the stick on the ice. "Butt-ending," that is, using the butt of your stick to hit an opponent, is also covered by this rule.

The above, with the exception of spearing, are usually "minor" penalties calling for the offending player to spend 2 minutes in the penalty box while his team plays short-handed. If the offending player has drawn blood, the minor penalty may be upgraded to a 5-minute major. Minor penalties are also called for playing with a broken stick (if you break a stick, drop it immediately), throwing a stick or having too many men on the ice.

Major Penalties

These are 5 minutes long and are generally called for *fighting*, *spearing* or *drawing blood*. During a major penalty the penalized team is not permitted to play at full strength for the full 5 minutes, regardless of how many times its opponents score. During a minor penalty, the penalized player may return to the ice if the opposing team scores once, even though the full 2 minutes have not elapsed.

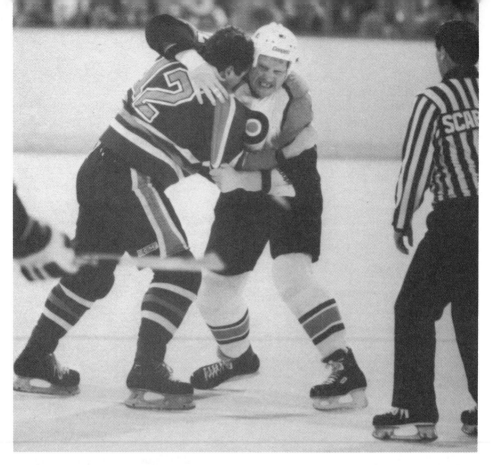

There is no place in hockey for fighting.

Misconduct brings a 10-minute penalty. It's often assessed for arguing too heatedly with an official. The penalized player must remain in the penalty box until the first stoppage of play following expiration of his 10 minutes, but his team does not have to skate short-handed.

Game Misconduct involves a suspension for the remainder of the game. It usually is handed out to a player who repeatedly attempts to fight, or to a player who intervenes (that is, is "third man") in a fight already in progress.

A penalty shot is the extraordinary and exciting call that gives a player the puck at center ice and allows him to skate in alone on the goaltender and attempt to score on a **single shot** (a goal on a rebound doesn't count). Penalty shots are generally awarded 1) when a player on a breakaway is tripped or otherwise pulled down from behind and fails to get a shot away; 2) when a defender, other than the goalkeeper, handles the puck in the crease; or, 3)—in a recent rule change in some leagues, including the NHL—when a defender stops play by deliberately dislodging his goal during the last 2 minutes of a game.

Even a clean game of hockey, played completely within the rules, still has the potential for injuries from falls, flying pucks, legal checks and accidental high sticks. For your own protection, and so you can play the game without undue concern for injury, don't take to the ice without the appropriate gear.

EQUIPMENT

Besides your skates, which we'll discuss in the next chapter, your stick is your most important piece of equipment. Goaltenders, of course, use a special stick—along with a lot of other special paraphernalia—which we will discuss in Chapter Seven, "Goaltending." For now, let's concentrate on the sticks and gear used by forwards and defensemen.

Sticks

Hockey sticks are designated either "left" or "right," according to the way the blade curves. If you are a left-handed shot—that is, if you prefer to hold the stick with your left hand lower on the shaft—you will want a blade curved so that your forehand passes and shots will be coming off the forward-curving part of your blade (see illustration).

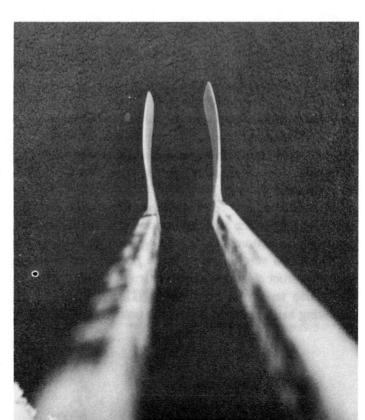

Left- and right-bladed hockey sticks.
The blade on the left is for a left-handed shot, the blade on the right for a righty.

While hockey sticks—like baseball bats, golf clubs and tennis rackets—must be selected with some regard for the intangible "feel," there are certain restrictions covering stick measurements and design. Your stick must not be more than 60 inches long from the heel to the top of the shaft, and not more than 12½ inches from the toe of the blade to the heel. The blade may not be less than 2 nor more than 3 inches wide, and its curvature—that is, how much the blade departs from a perfectly straight line—may not be more than one-half inch. A player caught using an illegal stick is subject to a minor penalty.

A short-shafted stick will offer you greater puck control while a long-shafted stick gives you the advantage of greater reach. To approximate the correct stick length for you, use the old "rule of chin." Stand barefoot, holding your stick so that it rests on the point of its toe. The top of the stick should reach your chin. If you are wearing skates, the top of the stick should be about three inches below your chin.

While you can adjust the length of your stick, the lie—the angle between the blade and the handle—cannot be adjusted and must be correct for you when you purchase the stick. The higher the lie number, the smaller the angle between the blade and the shaft, thus the easier it is to control the puck when it is close to your skates. The lower the lie number, the larger the blade-to-shaft angle and the easier it is to control the puck at a greater distance from your skates. Most players use lies 5 or 6 (manufacturers' standard sizes) though some professional and college players get custom-made lies of 4 or 7. You can't test for a suitable lie when buying a stick in a store. It is only by actually playing with a stick that you will be able to experiment and find out which lie is best for you.

Recent advances in stick design have seen the formerly universal wooden stick challenged by sticks made of fiberglass and, more recently, of aluminum shafts with replaceable fiberglass blades. Again, the material in your stick is a personal choice; some players are partial to what they claim is the greater "feel" (sensitivity) of wood, others, such as Wayne Gretzky, prefer the light weight of fiberglass, while others claim that the aluminum stick (like the aluminum baseball bat) gives them greater power on their shots.

No matter what type of stick you select, you should prepare it by taping a "grip" at the top of the shaft. In hockey, the top hand on your stick is your control hand while the bottom hand is your power hand. Since sticks are slippery, a taped grip offers you surer control. Some players prefer a small knob of tape while others construct elaborate spirals extending a foot or more down the shaft. You should also tape your stick blade. This will help you control the puck by cushioning hard passes as they come onto your stick and by minimizing the slip-

Parts of a Hockey Stick and Hockey-Stick "Lie"

Only by using a stick in practice and play will you find the lie that's right for you.

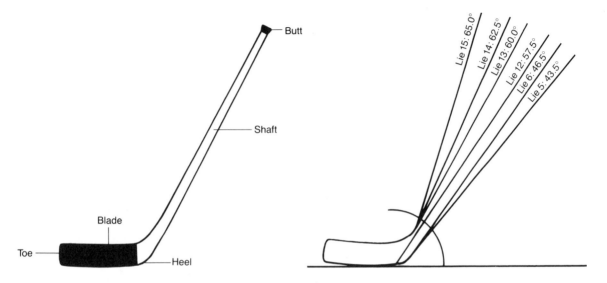

Taping a Hockey Stick

Taping the blade of a stick (left) helps both to preserve it and to provide a clearer target for teammates' passes. A knob of tape at the butt of the stick helps provide a surer grip (right).

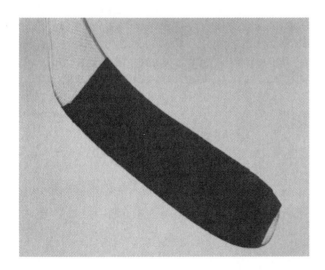

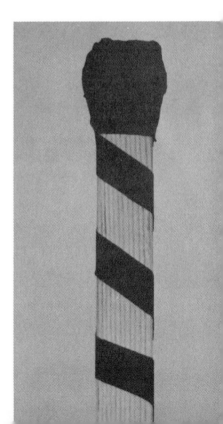

page of the puck against the blade when you stickhandle. Tape also reinforces the blade, helping to reduce stick breakage — an important consideration if you have to buy your own sticks. When taping the blade use *black* tape (some coaches insist on it); it will make your blade stand out against the white of the ice, creating a better target for teammates' passes.

Gloves

The thumb, palm and cuff are the most important variables to consider when buying gloves. You want solid protection around your thumb, the part of your hand most often hit by opponents' sticks. The palm of the glove must be soft and pliant to provide your hands with good stick "feel." The cuff must be strong enough to offer protection but should not extend so far up your arm that it reduces the flexibility of your wrists — a common problem for younger players too eager to move up to adult-size gloves. Some players improve wrist flexibility by undoing — or even completely removing — the glove lacings. If you do that, keep in mind that you are compromising the protective quality of the glove. If you do remove the lacings it is a good idea to wear a tennis-style wrist sweatband to guard against ice burn should the exposed part of your wrist get scraped along the ice.

Leg Guards

Gone are the days when old catalogs and magazines served as makeshift shin guards; today, knee protection is the key consideration in selecting leg guards. Choose a leg guard that offers not only a good knee cup pad but also ample wraparound padding to cover the sides of the knee and offer additional protection against ligament bruises. (When shopping for leg guards you'll discover that none has much effect on reducing ligament pulls or tears; for this reason, some players choose to wear football-style knee braces under their leg guards.) Your leg pads should also offer wide side flaps that will curve around your legs, protecting your calf muscles.

Elbow Pads

As in knee protection, you want an elbow pad that protects not only the point of the elbow but the sides as well.

Shoulder Pads and Chest Protectors

The basic shoulder pad will offer lightweight protection not only for your shoulders but also for your collarbone and upper arms. Recent design improvements have produced shoulder pads that include chest and back protection. While the amount of protection (and the corresponding increase in weight and decrease in flexibility) you want is an individual choice, defensemen are well advised to wear shoulder pad-chest protector combinations. The extra protection will give you more confidence in blocking shots.

Hip, Thigh, Kidney and Tailbone Pads

Most hockey pants are manufactured with pads built in. But in recent years, many players have begun wearing heavily padded girdles under their pants. The girdle fits so snugly that pads can't shift around as they can in a traditional hockey pant. The girdle pad is essential if your team is wearing the one-piece "overall" pant that comes with little or no built-in padding.

Protective Cup

The larger, heavily padded boxer-style cups are gaining popularity over the smaller, all-plastic cups. You'll probably find it most comfortable to wear the cup over a pair of shorts to reduce chafing on your legs. You should never go on the ice—even for a practice—without a protective cup.

Helmet and Mask

While players in the NHL have the option of wearing a helmet, players in junior, college, high school and youth leagues are now required to wear both helmets and face masks.

Do not purchase any helmet that does not bear the seal of approval of the Hockey Equipment Certification Council (HECC) or the Canadian Amateur Hockey Association. In addition, a list is available of that HECC-tested equipment approved by USA Hockey, which is its country's amateur hockey governing body (write USA Hockey, 4965 30 St., Colorado Springs, CO 80919).

Your choices in facial protection include 1) a plastic visor, 2) a wire cage-type mask or 3) a plastic visor/cage combination. The plastic visor—the kind you see on many NHL players—offers eye protection (though a stick can still get under

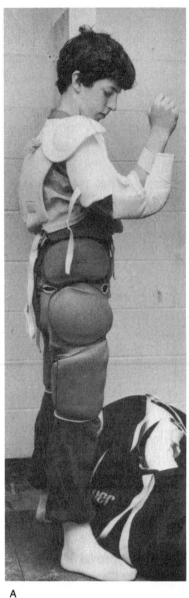

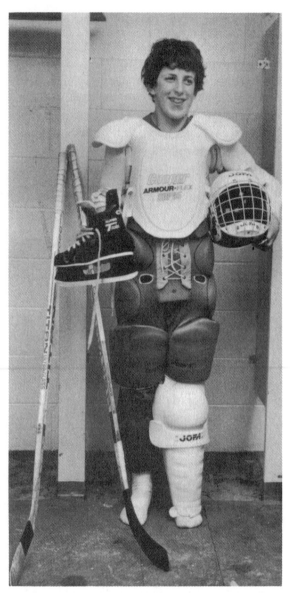

A

B

Protect yourself!
The shoulder pads you wear should offer thorough protection to your upper arms and backs of your shoulders. A heavily-padded girdle—worn under hockey pants—fits snugly so that padding won't shift out of place (A). Thigh, knee and shin guards along with a helmet and cage-type faceguard, (B) complete the basic protection that your head, trunk and legs need to avoid on-ice injury.

it) but does not protect your teeth and jaw. It is, therefore, almost exclusively confined to the professional leagues, with colleges, schools and youth leagues requiring full facial protection.

The wire cage mask (with a grid pattern tight enough to ward off the butt end of sticks) offers excellent protection but may interfere slightly with your vision.

The all-plastic visor/cage combination—with the visor protecting your eyes and a lower plastic cage portion to protect your jaw and teeth—facilitates breathing and offers excellent protection, now that manufacturers have largely solved the problem of the visor fogging up.

Whatever style you choose, have your helmet fitted by a qualified sporting goods dealer, and if the helmet and mask are purchased separately let the dealer attach them.

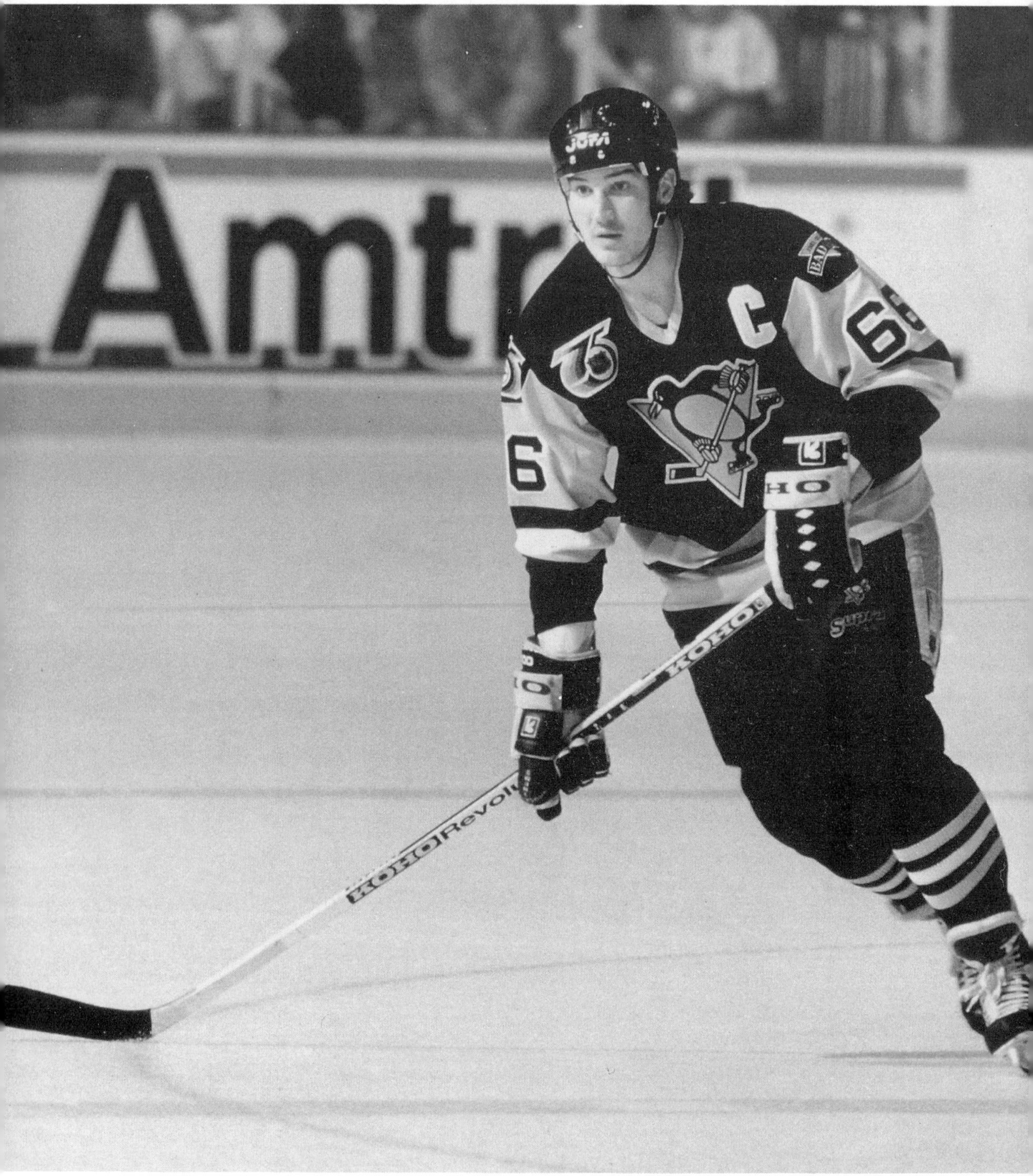
JOFA
Amtr
C
66
KOHO
KOHO Revol

2

Skating

In the beginning there is skating. It is a fundamental fact of your life as a hockey player that you will progress and improve only as far as your skating allows you. It doesn't matter that you can shoot a puck through quarter-inch plywood, stick-handle around three people in a phone booth or body-check opponents so hard that their helmets pop off. *If you can't skate you don't rate* — at least not as a hockey player.

Skating has always been hockey's single most important skill, and it's going to become even more important through the rest of the 1990s as our North American style of hockey continues to open up and speed up in response to Europe's influence on the game and to the success of such great skating professional teams as the NHL's Edmonton Oilers and Pittsburgh Penguins.

For example, already in today's game, wings and centers no longer skate only in prescribed lanes, as though they were mechanical men on rails, but interchange positions freely in the offensive zone and routinely skate back deep into the defensive zone. And defensemen's responsibilities no longer end at the offensive blue-line. Indeed, hockey defensemen are beginning to play more like basketball guards, triggering fast breaks and moving up to play important offensive roles. Even goalies, who used to wait for trouble to come to them, now commonly make their work easier and help their teammates by intercepting passes, clearing the puck and frequently going 10 to 20 feet out of the goal to make a breakout pass. All of these developments have taken hold in the last 10 years, and all share a common trait: a need for excellent skating ability.

Mario Lemieux's skating talents allow him to range
quickly and easily over the full length of ice.

POWER SKATING: AN OVERVIEW

For previous generations of hockey players, skating was learned more than it was taught. Players simply fell—oftentimes literally—into a skating style while playing in pick-up games on ponds, or in youth hockey games on town rinks. Not surprisingly, most players who learned in this haphazard manner became either "pond skaters" (smooth, freewheeling cruisers whose energy-conserving style was ideally suited to a three-hour Saturday afternoon skate on the lake but ill-suited to the up-tempo, stop-and-go pace of the modern game) or "ice choppers" (charging, high steppers who seemed to be running on their skates, squandering energy and tiring fast). But advances in skating instruction, beginning in the early '70s and continuing to the present day, have given rise to what is generally known as *power skating*—a system of instruction and drills designed to produce maximum technical efficiency in the three fundamentals of skating: stride, agility and endurance. Many teams, even at the NHL level, employ special coaches to teach power skating, and though the area of skating instruction is getting increasingly complex, the fundamentals of power skating are simple. Let's start from the bottom, with your skates.

SKATES

Skates are your most important piece of equipment and should be the best you can afford, even if that means economizing on other gear. To scrimp on your skates is to set artificial limits on your progress. The main considerations in choosing skates are boots and blades.

Boots

While some old-timers nostalgically bemoan the gradual disappearance of the all-leather skate boot, the fact is that modern boots, made of a combination of leather and stitched nylon or of molded plastic, offer better protection, fit and comfort. (Believe it, but don't expect your father to.) Generally speaking, a nylon and leather boot will fit 1 to 1½ sizes down from your shoe size, while molded plastic boots will usually conform to your shoe size. But you *must* try the skate on to ensure proper fit.

When trying on skates, wear the same socks you usually wear when skating. Most players prefer thin socks of cotton or light wool, which are absorbent yet thin enough to allow for a snug fit. A bulky sock reduces the amount of support

Skates.
Skates are your most important piece of equipment. The three types of hockey skates include (left) the goalie skate (note long blade for stability and plastic shell for protection); the nylon-and-leather-boot type (center), and the molded-plastic-boot type (right). Always buy the best skates you can afford—you won't be disappointed.

the boot can offer. Since your feet change sizes as you walk or exercise, the worst time to try on new skates is in the morning, when your feet are smallest.

Before lacing each new skate, sit down and kick your heel into the back of the boot. With your heel fitted snugly, your toes should extend flat and uncramped within the toe cap. As you lace the skate, keep kicking your heel back into the boot so that the lacings will be tightened evenly from bottom to top. A properly fitted boot requires firm lacing, not so tight that the lace cuts off circulation. If you find yourself lacing the skates extra tight for support, then the boots are either too big or poorly constructed. Whichever the case, *don't buy those skates!* Once you've laced both skates, stand up and walk around. Each foot should rest comfortably in its footbed and there should be no slippage in the heel.

Although a leather-and-nylon boot will stretch slightly after use, the material will mold around your foot if the boot fits properly. A word of warning: Never submerge stitched boots in water. This was once a popular method for breaking in all-leather boots—in fact, one ex-NHL player reportedly broke in new skates by wearing them into the shower. Instead, you can speed the break-in process by dampening your socks with hot water the first few times you skate. This will accelerate the normal perspiration soaking within the boot and help form it to the contours of your foot.

Parents should realize that children's skates must also fit snugly, even though that may mean buying a new pair of skates at least every year and possibly every six months, particularly for children between the ages of 4 and 11 whose feet grow at the rate of about one-third of an inch a year. The alternatives to buying perfectly fitted skates— 1) buying skates a size too large and letting the child grow into them, or 2) using hand-me-downs that may have little support left in the boot—will only handicap the child, undermining his self-confidence.

Double runners are also a bad idea. The boots on these skates rarely offer good support and the cheap blades won't cut the ice, causing the child to skid and totter about—and to lose heart with each inevitable fall.

Blades

While all high-quality boots come with blades attached (unlike figure skates, for which the boot and blade are often sold separately), even the best blade on the market will hinder your performance if it isn't properly prepared and sharpened. The three main considerations for ensuring optimum blade performance are: 1) the radius or rocker, 2) the lie and 3) the method of sharpening or grinding.

The term *radius* refers to the curvature in the blade and determines how much of the blade actually comes in contact with the ice. A long radius, one allowing about 5 or more inches of blade to touch the ice, will help produce an efficient stride and provide excellent stability, but it will limit your ability to cut and turn. A shorter radius, one allowing about 3 to 4 inches of blade to touch the ice, will offer great maneuverability but at the cost of somewhat reduced speed and stability. In general, a longer-radius blade is best if you're a novice skater, stability being your top priority. As you increase your skating ability and move up the hockey ladder, you will probably find that if you are a defenseman, you will want to stay with a longer-radius blade, while, if you're a forward, you will prefer a shorter radius. Goalies require almost no rocker on their blades since their primary need is stability.

Lie refers to the pitch of your blades and therefore determines your posture and weight distribution. A *negative lie* tilts your weight back on the blade, making you unbalanced and easy to knock over backward. A *neutral lie*, one that tilts you neither forward nor backward, is good for the average skater and preferred by some defensemen. A *forward lie* tilts your body weight forward, initiating motion but sacrificing some stability. Lie is a matter of personal preference, but chances are that even if you are defenseman, you will want a slight forward lie. Having your weight slightly forward helps you get off to quicker starts and aids your momentum as you stride toward top speed. And let's face it, you will be skating forward more frequently than you will be skating backward.

Sharpening

Establishing your radius, lie and blade sharpness is a job for a professional. Stay away from the hardware store that offers skate sharpening as a low-priority side-line. Take your skates to a pro shop or to a skate store employing an expert sharpener. Find out where figure skaters or the top hockey players in your area get their skates sharpened. That is probably where you should be going, especially for that crucial first sharpening.

Although it varies with individual preferences and skating styles, in general you will want your skates sharpened after every 4 to 8 hours of ice time. Proper sharpening means using the *hollow-ground system*, in which the middle of the blades are slightly hollowed, producing four edges—inside right, inside left, outside right and outside left—on which you can stop, push off or turn.

Care of Skates

When you remove your skates, loosen the lacings and pull back the tongue. That permits maximum air circulation, allowing the skate to dry thoroughly. If you're using molded plastic boots, take out the lining to allow it to dry. Always wipe your blades and rivets to prevent rusting. And use skate guards when you store your skates in your equipment bag or when you have to wear them across any surface other than ice or the rubber mats leading to the rink.

All right. You have a properly fitted and sharpened pair of skates. Now lace 'em up and let's head for the ice.

Skate guards.
Skate guards help ensure longer blade life.

THE MECHANICS OF POWER SKATING

The purpose of power skating is to help you produce maximum thrust from each skating stroke and achieve maneuverability without sacrificing balance.

Good skating requires proper posture, since all your skating motions flow from your initial stance. The most effective and comfortable posture includes having your legs about shoulder-width apart for balance, your knees flexed, your weight on the balls of your feet, your body bent slightly at the waist to assist in giving you a natural forward momentum, and your chest out and head up for ease in breathing. Keeping your head up also gives you a full view of the action in front of you, while skating with your head down for more than a fraction of a second makes you a target for a body check you probably won't see coming.

While the above describes a basic skating stance, you'll find that posture varies slightly by player and position. For example, Los Angeles center Wayne Gretzky has a pronounced bent-over style that gives him maximum speed. Though

In contrast to Rod Langway's upright skating posture (top), Wayne Gretzky skates in a crouch (bottom).

his head sometimes appears to be down, his eyes are up, scanning the play with his extraordinary peripheral vision. On the other hand, defensemen Doug Wilson of Chicago and Rod Langway of Washington prefer a more erect skating stance, as do many other defensemen who realize they must maintain a full overview of the rink and who often must shift from skating forward to skating backward. Eventually, you'll develop your own skating style, but that style should evolve from the fundamental mechanics.

The Start

It isn't how fast you go but how quickly you get there: A good start often determines whether you reach an opening on the ice (known in hockey as "hitting a hole") before it closes, win the race to a loose puck, or catch up to the player you are chasing before he becomes a dot on the horizon.

Forward from a Standing Start

The best position for a powerful takeoff—say, for all players on a faceoff situation—is to assume normal skating position with your forward skate (the one nearest the direction in which you want to go) turned slightly outward, ready for an explosive push-off. Your weight is on this forward skate. As you start, swing

Power Skating: The Stride

To start the stride, the skater has fully extended his right leg (A) for maximum thrust and then begins striding forward with his left leg. At the start of the new stroke, the player brings

A

B

your arm, shoulder and hip in the direction of the forward skate. *Drive* off that skate and quickly bring your rear skate forward. Beware of the common fault of lifting the rear skate too high, which wastes time and energy. As your rear foot moves forward, turn your toe outward so that you'll be prepared to push off again quickly when the blade hits the ice. The first few strokes after a start are short and explosive, differing from normal skating stride. Like a sprinter, you want to generate power before increasing your stride to its normal length.

Stride

Unlike the quick start—in which much of your power comes from your calf and thigh muscles—the most powerful and efficient skating stride is one that generates thrust mainly from the hips down. In the normal skating stride, you want your body bent forward from the hips, advancing your center of gravity and providing forward momentum for each stroke. As you stroke, you want your forward leg bent at the knee and your back leg—the one completing the stroke—completely extended, with the blade digging into the ice for maximum push. Failure to extend your back leg fully means you are skating mainly from the knees down instead of from the hips down, and thus are losing power. At the finish of a proper skating stroke, your rear foot should be facing almost at a right angle to the direction in which you are moving.

his rear leg forward quickly (B and C) and strides onto the blade of his forward skate while pushing hard off the rear skate (D).

C

D

As your front foot hits the ice to begin a new stroke, bring your rear leg forward quickly—initiating the forward action with your hip—keeping the skate as low to the ice as possible so that your motion is more a glide than a herky-jerky pick-them-up-and-lay-them-down action.

While most power comes from the hips and legs, your arms and shoulders are important for momentum and balance. In skating, your arms and shoulders move in sync with your legs—that is, your right arm and shoulder move forward and backward with the forward-backward movement of your right leg, your left arm and shoulder in rhythm with the forward-backward movement of your left leg. That is unlike running, in which your arms and shoulders move in opposition to your legs.

Power Skating: Front View

Here, the player has pushed off his right leg while striding forward with his left. Note that his hips, shoulders and arms are swinging to his left, adding momentum to his stride, and his head and eyes are *up* so that he can see the play in front of him and avoid body checks.

OTHER IMPORTANT SKATING TECHNIQUES

Stopping

Once you get beyond the beginner's inevitably painful though time-honored methods of stopping — A) falling, or B) slamming into the boards — you should master the three types of stops most frequently used in hockey: 1) the two-bladed stop, 2) the one-bladed stop, and 3) the backward stop.

The Two-Bladed Stop. This is the stop you see frequently in games, and even more often in publicity photos: A player moving at full speed comes to a sudden stop in a spectacular shower of ice chips.

To position yourself for a two-bladed stop you must turn your body and blades at right angles to the direction in which you were skating. As you turn, bend your knees and dig both blades into the ice, much as a skier would do. If you are turning and stopping to your left, then the inside edge of your right (or forward) skate and the outside edge of your left (or rear) skate will be shaving the ice. As you straighten your legs, your blades will dig deeply into the ice, bringing you to a stop. The most common fault in a two-bladed stop is some players' tendency to favor one side when stopping.

The two-bladed stop.
Here, the player stops by turning his blades at right angles to the direction in which he has been skating (A). He then digs into the ice with the inside edge of his forward skate and outside edge of his rear skate and stops (B).

A

B

A simple drill will help you avoid this natural bias. Practice stops and starts while skating from one blue line to the other, and make sure you face the same side of the arena each time you stop, ensuring that half your stops will be to the left and half to the right.

The One-Bladed Stop. This method of stopping involves the same principles as the two-bladed method but offers the advantage that, by stopping on one leg, you leave your other leg free to start off in a different direction. To make a one-bladed stop to the right, turn your body so that it faces to the right, press your weight forward on the inside edge of your left skate and, as you come to a stop on your left leg, your right leg will be free to begin a forward stride. Again, practice this stop equally on your left and right legs.

The one-bladed stop.
The advantage of this stop is that it leaves one leg free so that you can quickly begin a stride in a new direction. Here, the player stops by pressing his weight onto the inside edge of his forward skate. You can stop on your rear skate, too, but you will be off balance.

The Backward Stop. This is similar to the skier's snowplow stop except that it is performed in reverse. While skating backwards (more in a moment), point your toes out and your heels in, with your legs well bent at the knees. You stop by pressing the inside edges of both blades into the ice. You can also make a backward stop by pressing down on the inside edge of only one blade. As in the case of the one-bladed forward stop, this offers the advantage of keeping your other leg free to begin the next stride.

The backward stop.
Here, the player is pressing down on the inside edge of his rear (right) blade, leaving his left leg free to begin a pivot or a forward stride. You can also stop by pressing down on the inside edges of *both* skates in a kind of backward "snowplow" (right).

Crossovers

The term crossover refers to the movement of one leg in front of the other while you are skating through a turn. Crossing over helps you maintain balance and increase speed while turning.

Most players find it easier to cross over to the left than to the right, partly because many beginners practice at public skating rinks, where the flow of traffic is almost always counterclockwise. But a hockey player must learn to cross over both ways. Let's say you want to cross over as you skate clockwise behind the net. As you start your turn, get your body low, lean into the turn and keep your inside leg (right leg, in this case) well bent at the knee. Your outside (or left) leg is your power leg. Push off that outside leg, then whip it forward, crossing it over in front of your inside leg as you move through the turn.

Crossing Over

As the player skates through a turn, he pushes off his outside (right) leg (A) and transfers his weight to his inside leg (B). Then, as he continues through the turn, he brings his outside leg forward (C), crossing it over his inside leg. The crossover stride helps you gain speed on a turn.

A

One of the best ways of practicing crossovers is to skate figure-eights the length of the rink, turning behind both goals. That will force you to turn in both directions. You and your coach should make sure you use the crossover stroke both ways instead of crossing over only in the direction in which you feel comfortable and merely gliding when you have to turn the other way.

Skating Backwards

The ability to skate backwards is the most important skill a defenseman can have. But it is important for *all* players to be able to skate backwards with speed and balance.

Posture is crucial in backwards skating. Keep your buttocks down and your

B

C

Skating Backwards

D

This stride begins with the player pushing off the inside edge of his left skate (A) while gliding backwards on his rear skate (B). He then reverses the procedure, pushing off his right inside edge while gliding backward on his left skate (C,D). To improve his stability, the player performs these maneuvers in a slight crouch, as if he is about to sit in a chair.

C

B

A

knees well bent. The late legendary defenseman Eddie Shore used to compare the posture to the position of a person seated in a chair. If you assume too high a stance you will be easy to knock over and you won't be able to generate the kind of power that can come from pushing off well-bent knees. As you start skating backwards, drive the inside edge of one blade into the ice and straighten that leg to provide your backward thrust. Then transfer your weight to your other leg and do the same. You gain speed by swinging your hips side to side in coordination with your legs. Indeed, hip sway is a natural motion in backwards skating, but most of your power must come from your leg thrust and you should avoid using an exaggerated butt swing to try to gain speed. You won't generate that much power and you'll look ridiculous trying to "wag your tail."

Backward Crossovers

Like the forward crossover, you will have to learn to execute backward crossovers in both directions, and, here again, the figure-eight is a good drill. The action in a backward crossover is the same as in a forward crossover in that you cross your outside leg in front of your inside leg. For example, if you were doing backward crossovers clockwise, your right (or outside) foot would be moving in front of your left (or inside) foot as you move backward through the turn.

Pivoting

All players, particularly defensemen, must be able to pivot from skating forward to skating backward, or vice versa, and do it with the least possible loss of time, speed and balance. A defenseman who is too slow in pivoting will be beaten repeatedly by opposing forwards.

Forward to Backward. The key to a good pivot is quick, confident weight transfer. Suppose you are skating forward—say, into your defensive zone—and want to turn around and skate backward to face the oncoming attack. For the sake of this example, further suppose that you want to turn counterclockwise. As you stride forward on your left skate, you will naturally transfer your weight to that skate. At the end of that stride—with your left leg supporting you—swing your hips, shoulders and right leg in the direction you want to turn, (here, counterclockwise). As you do that, your left foot will pivot 180 degrees and you will end up facing the direction from which you just came. As soon as you complete the pivot, get your free skate (right skate, in this case) down on the ice for balance and for power as you begin to skate backwards.

Backward to Forward. Suppose that you are skating backwards when an opponent suddenly dumps the puck into the corner and you have to turn, skate forward and beat him to it. Let's say the puck is in the right corner and you have to pivot clockwise to your right. Again, the pivot is made on one blade, in this case your right. As you skate backward and transfer your weight to your right foot, whip your hips, shoulders and free (left) leg in the direction you want to turn, (clockwise). As you pivot on your right skate, keep your free left leg high and well bent at the knee so that, the instant it hits the ice, you are in position for your first forward stride and thus for a good start in that race for the puck.

A good drill for practicing forward and backward pivots is to skate the length of the rink, goal line to goal line. Skate forward to the first blue line, pivot and skate backward to the center red line. Again, pivot and skate forward to the far

Pivoting (Backward to Forward)

The key to successful pivoting is quick, confident weight transfer. Here, the player, skating backwards (A), begins a clockwise pivot by transferring his weight onto his rear leg (B and

A   B   C

blue line, pivot, and skate backward to the end of the rink. Be sure to alternate the direction of your pivots: If your first forward-to-backward pivot is clockwise, make sure the next one is counterclockwise.

Nothing is as important to hockey as good skating, and nothing is as important to skating as constant practice. This chapter has covered the fundamentals of skating, but a good course in power skating, attendance at a hockey camp that includes instruction in power skating, or just a lot of hard work on your own will help you translate your technical knowledge into speed, agility and endurance.

Hockey is really two sports in one, and as your skating improves so will your game. Now let's look at two other basic skills you'll need to master to be a complete hockey player: stickhandling and passing.

C). With all his weight there, he is free to turn his body (D) and finally to whip his rear (left) leg around to start a new stride (E).

D

E

3

Stickhandling and Passing

Once you begin to feel comfortable as a skater, you're ready to build on that foundation and to begin learning the other skills common to the game, the most important of which are stickhandling—the art of advancing the puck with your stick—and passing. Of course shooting (which we will discuss in the next chapter) is an important skill, too, but, let's face it, neither you nor your teammates will create many chances to shoot if you can't control the puck with your stickhandling and passing. Indeed, as any coach will tell you, to control the puck is to control the game. Before you gain control of the puck, however, you must have control of your stick.

CONTROLLING THE STICK

The Grip

Control of the stick begins with the proper grip. Your top hand—which, remember, is your control hand—is placed over the taped knob at the top of the stick shaft. Not surprisingly, many righthanded players are left shots, preferring to have their more dexterous hand in the control position.

Your lower hand is your power hand, though that doesn't mean you're supposed to use it to try to squeeze sap out of the stick. Grip your stick much as you would a golf club, that is, with most of the pressure in your fingers rather than in your palms. That will give you a better feel for the puck. Remember that while the standard grip for stickhandling has your hands fairly high on the stick—roughly 16 to 18 inches apart—you will be lowering your bottom hand slightly for passing and even further for shooting.

53

With his head up, hands in their proper position on the stick and the stick blade cupping the puck as he dribbles it from side to side, Wayne Gretzky has everything in control as he moves up the ice.

FUNDAMENTAL STICKHANDLING MANEUVERS

Stickhandling is basically the art of passing the puck to yourself as a means of advancing it through traffic while protecting it from opponents. The most fundamental stickhandling maneuver is the side-to-side dribble.

The Side-to-Side Dribble

In this, as in all stickhandling moves, you want to keep the puck in the middle of your stick blade. As you move the puck from side to side, cup the blade over the puck to keep it from bouncing over the blade and to protect it from your opponents. For quickness and fluidity in stickhandling, keep your elbows well out from your body and your hands and wrists as loose and flexible as possible. The often-heard term "cement hands" is appropriate for a player who habitually holds his stick so tightly that he loses control of the puck.

When first practicing the side-to-side dribble you might find it helpful to stand still and simply slide the puck from left to right, and right to left, catching it with your stick. When you feel you have the puck under control, try the same maneuver while skating. At first you will have to look at the puck to control it. But, as quickly

Cupping the puck.
Always cup your stick blade over the puck (A,B) when making and receiving passes and when stickhandling. This keeps the puck from accidentally sliding up and over your blade and also protects it from opponents. You can and should cup the blade on your backhand side, too (C).

A   B   C

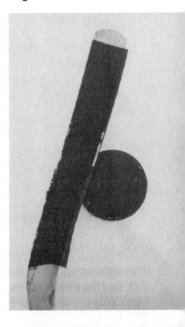

The Side-to-Side Dribble

Stickhandling is basically the art of passing the puck to yourself. In the side-to-side dribble shown here, note that the player keeps the puck in the center of his stick blade and that the blade is cupped over the puck, both as he begins his dribble (A and F) and as he receives his own "pass" (C and H). At all times the player keeps his head up and maneuvers the puck by feel.

A

B

C

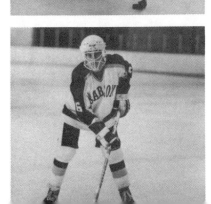

D

E

F

G

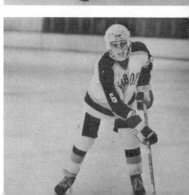

H

as possible, you must teach yourself to stickhandle *without looking at the puck*. "Keep your head up" is one of the cardinal rules of hockey. If you persist in stick-handling with your head down, you not only will be unable to see passing and shooting opportunities, you will also make yourself a sitting duck for a crunching body check.

The Forward-and-Back Dribble

This is more difficult than the side-to-side dribble but it is a move you must perfect because it is particularly useful in making a defender commit himself. With the puck pushed well ahead of you and seemingly out there for grabs, your opponent will often make a lunge for it, putting himself off balance and giving you a chance to pull the puck back and skate around him.

The forward-and-back dribble is similar to the side-to-side dribble insofar as

The Forward-and-Back Dribble

In this dribble you keep the puck at your side—that is, in a position where you can pass or shoot it. Here, the stickhandler brings the puck forward (A,B), cups his blade protectively

A

B

you keep the puck in the center of your blade and cup the blade over the puck when you draw it back. One major difference between the two dribbles lies in the hand action. In pushing the puck forward in a forward-to-back dribble, some players let go of the stick with their bottom hand and, for a second or so, control the stick only with their top hand. Try it yourself. You'll see that releasing your lower hand from the stick allows you to push the puck ahead a greater distance. However, as you draw the puck back toward your body, you must remember to get that bottom hand back on your stick for better control. Stickhandling one-handed is not a good idea, except for very brief periods when you need that extra reach.

In general, you should also know when NOT to stickhandle. Don't try stickhandling when you are the last man back (if you lose the puck you'll give up a breakaway), and don't waste time stickhandling if you see you can advance the play safely and faster by passing to an open teammate.

over the puck (C), then pulls the puck back (D,E). As in the side-to-side dribble, the puck is on the center of the blade and the player's head and eyes are up.

C   D   E

STICKHANDLING DRILLS

The simplest stickhandling drill, and thus the best one for beginners involves practicing the two basic dribbles (side-to-side and forward-and-back) while standing still.

The Slalom Drill

After you've mastered the two basic dribbles, you or your coach can set up a kind of slalom course using rubber pylons or any objects that will force you to dribble the puck right and left as you thread your way through the course.

The slalom drill.
To improve both your stickhandling *and* your skating, try skating through a "slalom course" of rubber cones or similar markers while concentrating on the fundamentals of good stickhandling—keeping your head up, your stick cupped and your puck in the center of your stick blade.

The Against-the-Grain Drill

There is an excellent team drill to help you and your teammates learn to stick-handle with your heads up while moving the puck through traffic. Players begin dribbling a puck around the rink. All players are skating in the same direction. Without warning, the coach calls out the names of three or four players who then must skate in the opposite direction—against the grain—keeping control of their pucks while avoiding collisions with the oncoming majority of players.

Keepaway

Finally, there is hockey's version of the old schoolyard game. Here, one person tries to keep control of the puck while any number of other players try to steal it. There will be many instances in which the player with the puck will have to use the forward-and-back dribble to freeze his opponents before he slips around them.

Street Hockey

Several NHL stars, among them retired Montreal great Guy Lafleur, have credited street hockey (or road hockey as it's sometimes called in Canada) with improving their stickhandling skills. If you try it, you'll discover it takes a more delicate touch to maneuver a bouncing ball across a rough surface than it does to sweep a flat-sided puck across a smooth sheet of ice.

PASSING

As hockey evolved, moving from the vast open spaces of frozen ponds and rivers into the relatively small confines of boarded rinks, it became less of a game for the individual virtuoso and more of a team sport. It is one thing to be able to out-skate or outstickhandle your opponents when you have acres of open ice to work with; it is another, and nearly impossible thing, to do it on a modern hockey rink. Try it, and your opponents will either converge on you in overwhelming numbers, finally stripping away the puck, or funnel you toward the boards where you will not have the room to use your speed or stickhandling skills. Thus, the ability to move the puck by passing has become a tactical necessity and a fundamental skill.

Only rarely can the defensive team shut off all passing routes to all targets. The real art and genius of passing lies not in the technical execution but in first seeing the best possible move, the one that will advance (or at least preserve) your team's position. Once again, we come back to the first rule of hockey: Keep Your Head Up. (I can't repeat the rule too often.) You may not be gifted with the wrap-around vision of a Wayne Gretzky or a Mario Lemieux, but a comprehensive look at the play around you is basic to sound passing. Here, as in stickhandling, you must get used to making all the different types of passes without looking down at the puck.

The Forehand Pass

Before attempting this or any pass, make sure you have total control of the puck. As in stickhandling, the puck should be positioned in the middle of your blade and the blade cupped over the puck.

The forehand pass—the easiest pass to make and receive—is best used when you have no need for deception and when you have time. In making a forehand pass, you want to sweep the puck *forward* toward the target, that is, your team-mate's stick blade. Make sure your blade stays on the ice as you release the puck.

The Forehand Pass

This is the easiest pass to execute and to receive. As he sweeps the puck forward, the

A

B

If your stick leaves the ice, chances are the puck will, too, and your pass will be hard to control.

The Flip Pass

You use the flip pass when all the on-ice routes are closed and you have to lift the puck a few inches to clear an opponent's stick or several feet to get it over a sprawled body. To make a flip pass, use a quick upward snap of your wrists and a high follow-through. What you're trying to do is get your stick blade under the puck to loft it over the obstacles in front of you, much like a wedge shot in golf. If time allows, you can make this shot easier to execute by drawing the puck back toward you, as you do in the forward-and-back dribble. That will bring the puck tight against your blade and make it easier for you to get the tip of your blade under the puck, to obtain the needed elevation.

It is an advanced play, but a flip pass out of your defensive zone—high enough to go over the heads of opposing defensemen but soft enough to land in neutral ice where one of your teammates can collect it—is one way of setting up breakaways.

passer looks at his target, not at the puck (A,B). As it leaves the passer's stick (C), the puck is *flat on the ice*, and the follow-through is low and directed at the target (D).

C

D

A

B

The Flip Pass

Here, the idea is to get your stick blade *under* the puck in order to launch the pass in the air. The passer begins by sweeping the puck forward (A). Then, with his stick blade tight

The Backhand Pass

The backhand pass is more difficult than the forehand pass because, as you sweep your stick in a backhand movement, there is a tendency for your lower arm and body to rise, lifting your stick off the ice. The key to a good backhand pass is

A

B

The Backhand Pass

The key to a successful backhand pass is keeping your lead shoulder *down* as you move the puck forward on your backhand. Here, the passer keeps his left shoulder down (A,B), then releases the puck toward the receiver (C), and follows through (D). If you lift your lead shoulder, you might scoop your blade under the puck, inadvertently lifting the pass off the ice.

C

D

against the puck, he makes a quick, powerful flip of his wrists, forcing the blade under the puck (B) and lifting the pass off the ice (C). Note his follow-through: higher than that for an on-ice pass.

to *keep your lower shoulder down* so that your blade—and, thus, the puck—stays on the ice. All players, but especially centers who have to pass equally well to their left and right, should be able to make quick, accurate backhand passes.

C

D

The Drop Pass

Here the player on the left simply leaves, or "drops" the puck behind him (A,B) where his teammate, moving in from the right, can easily pick it up (C).

A

The Drop Pass

There are times when an attacking player can gain a momentary advantage in space and time by playing the puck back to a trailing teammate. The most effective way to gain that advantage is with a drop pass.

Let's say you are skating at a defenseman in your attacking zone. The defenseman has good position on you and there is no teammate ahead of or even with you to whom you can pass the puck. But there *is* a teammate moving into the zone behind you. This is the perfect time for a drop pass. You make this pass—which isn't really a pass at all but rather an abandoning of the puck—by putting your stickblade in front of the puck to stop its forward motion while you continue to skate forward, leaving the puck nearly motionless behind you. Your teammate should be able to move in, collect the loose puck and get off a shot before the defenseman has time to recover. *Be careful not to push the puck backwards fast.* When you see a drop pass executed in a college or a pro game, it often happens so fast that it appears the passer is actually passing backwards. But what happens on a properly executed drop pass is that the passer leaves the puck, giving it only the *slightest* backward movement, or "tail", almost as though he had made a mistake and overskated it.

Leading the Receiver

As you practice passing you will also have to work on developing a feel for "leading" your teammate with the pass in much the same way that a football quar-

B

C

terback leads his receiver. This means estimating your receiver's speed (how fast he is going when you make the pass) and his range (how far he can go at top speed) so that you pass not to where he is but to where he is going to be or, more appropriately, to where his *stick blade* is going to be. And keep in mind that receiving a pass can be a difficult job, so don't make your pass any harder than is necessary. There will be times when defensive pressure forces you to pass the puck quickly and hard but, given a choice, a slower pass that the receiver can "skate onto" (that is, catch up with) is better than a hard pass that the intended receiver may not be able to handle.

Pass Receiving

Think of pass receiving not as "stopping" the puck, but as "catching" it with your stick.

As a pass comes to you, resist the natural inclination to tighten the grip on your stick. Instead, make sure your stick is facing the direction from which the pass is coming and stay loose. Keep your hands soft, relaxed. Don't squeeze the stick. Tilt or cup your stick blade so that, when you receive the pass, the puck will not go bouncing over or off your stick. As the puck makes contact with your blade, *give with the pass.* By moving your stick back with the puck you "cushion" the pass, reducing the likelihood of the puck's bouncing away from you. Stay calm and don't reach for the puck. Always receive a pass with your stick at right angles to the path of the approaching puck.

Pass Receiving

The player about to receive a pass keeps his eyes on the puck (A), following it all the way onto his stick (B), in the same way as a football receiver "looks" the ball into his hands. When puck and stick make contact, the receiver "gives" with the puck (C) to bring it under control and to prevent it from bouncing off his stick.

A

PASSING DRILLS

There are a great many passing drills (coaches probably have more drills for passing than for any other skill) but a few time-tested ones, useful for learning fundamentals, are:

"Playing Catch"

In this basic drill, you and a teammate stand 20 to 30 feet apart and simply pass the puck back and forth, just as though you were playing catch with a baseball. Concentrate on using proper passing and receiving technique—don't slap the puck back and forth. Start with slow passes and gradually pick up the tempo. Remember, even the hardest passes, if properly received, should not bounce off your stick blade. Practice all possible combinations: forehand to forehand, forehand to backhand, backhand to forehand, backhand to backhand.

Passing While Skating

After you perfect your technique in a stationary drill, you and your teammate can skate down the ice side by side, passing the puck back and forth. The player receiving the puck should stickhandle it (that is, dribble it from side to side) once to gain full control and to prevent a useless kind of ping-pong passing that players

B   C

can fall into when they simply want to get rid of the puck as opposed to truly "passing" it. You and your partner should switch sides frequently so that you get a chance to work on both forehand and backhand passing and receiving.

The Flip-Pass Drill

The flip-pass drill is similar to "playing catch" except now a stick or similar obstacle is placed between you and your partner, and the two of you practice flipping the puck over it. Concentrate on trying to make your passes land flat on the ice so they will be easier for the receiver to control.

Lead Pass, Drop Pass

This is a good drill for working on two passes at once. Start at one end of the ice about 20 feet behind a teammate who will be your receiver. Make a *lead pass* up to your teammate, then skate behind him into the offensive zone. Your teammate (who, of course, enters the zone first to be onside) skates about 20 feet into the attacking zone and leaves a drop pass for you, which you collect for an immediate shot on goal. Now reverse positions and go back up ice, with your teammate making a lead pass to you, and you leaving him the puck on a drop pass for the shot on goal.

    When making your lead pass, concentrate on putting the puck on the

Edmonton's Paul Coffey (right) executes a perfect lead pass to Mark Napier.

receiver's forehand side (so he can handle it easily) and on leading him enough so that he can collect the pass in full stride. When making your drop pass, remember not to push the puck back fast (or your receiver may overskate it).

Circle Keepaway

In this drill, six or seven players form a circle—roughly the size of a faceoff circle—with one or two players in the middle. The players forming the circle pass the puck around randomly while the player(s) in the middle try to deflect or intercept the passes. When either an interception or deflection occurs, the player who made the unsuccessful pass goes to the middle of the circle while the player who deflected or intercepted it takes his place on the edge of the circle. This drill forces players 1) to make quick, crisp, accurate passes to both forehand and backhand, 2) to receive passes smoothly, and 3) to look before passing. The built-in competition maintains players' interest and makes this drill fun.

As you practice, the mechanics of stickhandling and passing will gradually become second nature. But keep in mind that it is not mechanics that makes the excellent hockey player. It is the ability to perform these skills at top speed and without looking down at the puck that separates the truly accomplished player from the merely mechanically competent. When you have played and practiced so much that you can handle the puck by feel, then you will be free to look at the play around you and decide if it is best to advance the puck by stickhandling or by passing. When you combine that ability with a solid foundation in skating, then you have all the individual tools you need to work with your teammates in moving the puck into position for a shot on goal—which, of course, is what this game is all about.

4

Shooting

If you look at an NHL scoring sheet you will see that, in most games, even the top scorers will have only two or three shots on goal, and several players may have one, or even none. In general, a team will get 30 to 40 shots per game. If each team takes 30 shots (60 shots total) and each shot takes one second (in actuality it would take less time), that means a game will consist of *one minute* of shooting and 59 minutes of trying to move the puck into position for a shot or preventing the other team from shooting. Yet the outcome of the game will inevitably depend on how well you or your opponents use those few precious seconds you get in which to put shots on goal. Scoring is the only way to win, and shooting is the only way to score. Shooting accurately, quickly and hard is the best way to score consistently.

Shooting, as a skill, differs from skating, passing and stickhandling in that you rarely get a chance to work on it during a game. Even superior forwards seldom get as many as five shots in a game. Thus, your progress as a shooter depends almost entirely on the time and effort you put into practicing, and hardly at all on game experience.

Since the act of shooting is intrinsically satisfying and fun, most players don't mind working on their shots. In fact, most hockey players would rather shoot a puck than work on any other skill. The problem is that a lot of this so-called shooting practice often amounts to little more than blasting the puck at the net or boards with too much emphasis on power and not enough attention to the other two important elements of effective shooting: accuracy and quick release.

The five basic shots are the forehand shot, the snap shot, the slap shot, the flip shot and the backhand shot. When you work on any of them, make sure that you have a target to aim at and that you concentrate on the sound mechanical execution that will, when perfected, allow you to get your shot away quickly.

71

Shooting is the only way to score and scoring is the
only way to win.

THE FOREHAND SHOT

The standard forehand wrist shot—or "sweep shot" as it is sometimes called—is the most common shot in hockey and probably the best shot for combining power and accuracy. It is particularly effective on middle-distance shots, say from 10 to 40 feet out from goal. Because your stick blade is in contact with the puck throughout the shooting motion (as opposed to the slap shot, in which there's only a millisecond of contact) it is difficult for the goalie to know exactly when you will release the shot or where it is going. This is the main reason most goals are scored on forehand shots.

To start this shot, keep the puck toward the heel of your stick, cup the stick blade over the puck, and draw the puck back, past your body. As you draw the puck back, slide your lower hand down the stick shaft. This lowered grip will give you greater power.

The forehand shot is characterized by a smooth, swift, sweeping motion for-

The Forehand Shot

Note the puck's position: toward the heel of the shooter's blade (A). Note, too, that the left hand is slightly lower on the shaft than it would be for stickhandling. As the player brings

D

C

ward. As you sweep the puck forward you want to transfer most of your weight onto your forward leg and keep enough downward pressure on your stick so that your shot will have some power to it. Look where you are shooting, don't stare down at the puck. As the puck moves past your body, snap your wrists forward, HARD, sending the shot on its way. Now follow through so that the blade of your stick ends up pointing at the target. Unlike the golfer who may select from a series of clubs—from the flat-hitting 1-iron to the high-lofting wedge—to get the shot height he wants, in hockey you must produce varying lofts using the same "club," your stick. You do this by adjusting your follow-through. A low follow-through means a relatively flat blade angle and a low trajectory. A high follow-through raises the angle and produces more loft.

When shooting a forehand shot, be careful not to make these two common errors:

1. *Shooting off the wrong foot.* When in the act of shooting you want to be

the puck forward, his eyes are on the target (B). His weight is transferred to his outside leg (C) as he releases the puck, then follows through (D).

B

A

Shooting off the wrong foot. Shooting off the foot nearest the puck leads to poor form and a weak, inaccurate shot.

transferring your weight to your forward or "outside" foot (right foot for a left shot, left foot for a right shot). This gives you a wide base of support, since some of your weight is on your stick and some is on your outside leg. It also means you are striding into your shot and can therefore shoot more powerfully. To shoot with your weight on the wrong foot—the inside foot—is to put yourself off balance. In effect, you will be leaning to the left if you are a left shot or the right if you are a right shot. You can be knocked over easily and will not be in position to get much body weight into your shot.

2. *Pulling up and away.* Beware of the natural tendency to raise your head and shoulders as you release the puck. As in a golf shot, you want to keep your body and, thus, your weight, over the puck until *after* you have shot it. Pulling up and away will produce a weak, inaccurate shot.

THE SNAP SHOT

While the standard forehand sweep shot is hard and accurate, it does have two disadvantages: 1) It takes time and 2) it takes space—the several feet required to sweep the puck forward to get the shot away. The snap shot—a quick-release version of the basic forehander—eliminates these disadvantages at the cost of only a slight loss in power and accuracy. The snap shot is a good move for capitalizing on those "half chances" to score that often materialize out of scrambles in front of the net, and for taking advantage of a goalie before he has time to set up.

In the snap shot, you don't draw the puck back, past your body, as you do in a forehand shot. Instead, you shoot without a wind-up. With the puck at your side and your wrists cocked, you snap your wrists to send the shot on its way. You gain the most from a snap shot by learning to take it while in full skating stride, saving the time otherwise needed to stop and plant your legs. The key to the shot is wrist strength for the powerful snap. The other mechanics are the same as in the forehand sweep shot—LOOK where you are shooting, follow through toward the target and keep your weight on your *outside* foot.

THE SLAP SHOT

This is the most controversial shot in hockey. Most players love it because it is a spectacularly powerful shot that brings gasps of admiration from spectators. Many coaches dislike it (one high school coach in Massachusetts once went so far as to ban its use by his players) because it is notoriously inaccurate and comparatively easy for a defenseman to block or for a goalie to save. Though the slap shot does have its limitations and is probably overused, it also has its appropriate uses and should be mastered by all players, particularly defensemen who are apt to use it frequently when shooting from the blue line.

To take a slap shot, 1) bring your stick back to roughly waist height or slightly higher (a full 180-degree windup only wastes time), 2) drop your lower hand about 6 to 8 inches down the shaft to get more weight into the shot and 3) swing downward, aiming not at the puck but at a point on the ice about an inch or two *behind* the puck. You want your stick to hit the ice first—hit it so hard there will be a slight bend in the shaft—and then explode into the puck. Keep your grip, particularly your bottom hand, tight so that there will be no give and therefore no loss of power when you make contact with the puck. For maximum power, transfer your weight to your outside foot as you make contact, that is—"stride into" the shot just as you would a powerful forehand. All other principles are the same as for the forehand shot—weight on your forward leg, follow through toward the target and don't pull up.

One of the best places for shooting a slap shot is the offensive blue line, particularly the "point." The "point," in hockey terminology, is not a particular spot on the ice but rather the location of a defenseman on the attacking blue line. The right defenseman is said to be on one point, the left defenseman on the other. When one of them shoots from the blue line it is often referred to as "a shot from the point." On the blue line, you are at least 60 feet from the goal, a rather long dis-

A   B

The Slap Shot

You'll get this shot off quicker if your backswing is only slightly above waist height (A) rather than all the way over your head. On the downswing, note that the shooter transfers his

ance one at which most wrist shots would lose much of their power before reaching the net. The slap shot will get the puck there in a hurry and, even though your windup automatically telegraphs the shot to the goaltender, you might still beat him by the sheer force of the shot, much as some pitchers do who can blow their fastballs past hitters even though the hitters know it's coming.

For similar reasons, the slap shot can also be useful when you are forced into shooting from a bad angle. Even though the goaltender might seem to have the goal mouth thoroughly protected, a powerful slap shot might still force its way between his pads or deflect in off his equipment.

Finally, one of the best situations for the slap shot is when you are shooting off a pass — that is, when you quickly slap an approaching pass at the net without taking the time to stop the puck first. This is called "one-timing" and it's a move that gives the goalie almost no chance to get set. Jari Kurri, right wing for the Los Angeles Kings, is one of the best in the world at taking slap shots off the pass, frequently blasting teammate Wayne Gretzky's passes into opponents' goals.

C   D

weight to his forward foot and that his stick hits the ice a few inches behind the puck (B). Note the bend of the stick shaft (C), indicating the power behind this shot. A low follow-through (D) produces a low, hard (and hard-to-save) shot on goal.

THE FLIP SHOT

This is a scorer's shot, one that sacrifices the power needed for long or intermediate shots to obtain the loft and accuracy required when shooting for the top corners of the net from close range, particularly when you have to lift your shot up and over a sprawled goalkeeper.

The flip shot, like the flip pass, starts with a short backswing. You cock your wrists and bring the top edge of your stick blade well forward. *Unlike* the flip pass, however, the flip shot requires that you uncock your wrists with much greater force to flip the puck upward. Make no mistake: The flip shot is never a powerful shot. But you do want to get the puck to the target as quickly as possible. (By contrast, the flip pass is more of a finesse maneuver since you want the puck to drop gently to the ice near the receiver.)

The Flip Shot

A

B

This is the perfect shot for lifting the puck over a sprawling goalkeeper. Here, the shooter keeps the puck toward the toe of his stick blade (A) as he sets to shoot. A quick, powerful flick of the wrists lifts the puck over the bench (B) (which can simulate a goalie in this drill) and sends it toward the top of the goal.

Position of the stick and puck for a quick, fast-rising flip shot.

Backhand shots may lack the power of forehand shots, but they have a high scoring ratio because they often catch the goalie by surprise. They also rise sharply, so that even when a goalie is set, he often can't judge the height of the shot until well after the puck has left the shooter's stick.

The backhand is a sweeping type of shot that in many ways is the reverse of the standard forehand sweep shot. In taking a backhand shot, start with the puck well behind your body and on the backhand side: your right side if you are a left shot and vice versa. Next lower your bottom hand on the stick about 12 inches and then sweep the puck forward in a kind of pulling motion, being careful to keep your leading shoulder down and turned toward the target. Most of the power on your backhand comes from the pulling force of that lead shoulder. For a low shot, release the puck near your feet; for a high shot, release it further in front of you.

While the advent of the curve-bladed stick has made the backhand more difficult and, therefore, less common, it has not made the shot impossible, as some coaches and texts have suggested. The curve on a stick blade is often more pronounced near the toe of the blade, leaving several inches of nearly straight surface near the heel. When taking a backhand shot, keep the puck down near the heel of your stick. That will reduce the risk of "roll-offs" due to the blade's curvature, and will add more power to your shot.

The backhand.
The backhand requires a pulling motion to be successful. Here, the shooter sweeps the puck forward (A), being careful to keep his lead shoulder down in order to keep the puck from rising too high. The shooter transfers his weight onto his lead foot and keeps his follow-through low as he sends his backhander into the goal (B).

B

A

WHERE TO SHOOT

Surveys of where goals are scored from show that most scoring shots are taken from an area between the faceoff circles and about 15 to 20 feet in front of the net. A shot from this area—usually called "the slot"—means you have a choice of hitting any of the four corners of the net. The goalie can't cover them all. When shooting from this prime scoring area, the best places to direct your shots, in order of their likelihood of success, are: 1) low to the goalie's stick side (because the goalie can only use his stick and skate and cannot catch the puck), 2) low to the goalie's glove side (goalies often carry their glove high to protect the top corner and are therefore vulnerable on a low shot), 3) high to the goalie's stick side (where he cannot catch the puck), or 4) high to his glove side. You can also score in what some players call "the five hole," that being the somewhat sizable gap some goalies leave between their legs. Since most goalies can move their hands faster than they can move their feet, low shots have the best chance of success.

As you move out of the prime scoring area you will have fewer shooting-location choices. In general, a shot from out on the right wing should be directed at the left side of the net, where the target will be largest. The only exception to this would be if a goaltender is badly out of position and has given you a big opening between his body and the near post—what hockey players call "the short side."

The Five Prime Scoring Areas

From easiest (1) to most difficult (5).

If you are forced to shoot long—say, from 40 feet or more—your best bet is a low slap shot. If there is a lot of traffic in front of the net it will be hard for the goalie to see the puck and, even if he can see it, it may be possible for a teammate to re-direct the puck, tipping it into the goal. Occasionally, these long shots will bounce into the net off the body of a defending player for a "gift goal."

After you take a shot, don't stand around admiring it. Follow it up by moving toward the goal and looking for a rebound.

The Shooting Angle

Because you shoot from the side of your body, the angle at which you view the net is not the same angle of the puck to the goal. When considering where to place your shot, try to view the goal from the angle of the puck—in other words, try to imagine how the puck would see the goal if the puck had eyes—and then shoot accordingly.

If you're at a bad shooting angle, say, deep in the corner, but there is no teammate to receive a pass and little chance for you to move to a better shooting position, don't be afraid to shoot. Even a shot from a bad angle is better than no shot at all or, as Wayne Gretzky once put it, "one hundred percent of the shots you don't take don't go in."

DEFLECTIONS

Re-directing a hard shot or pass into the goal is one of the most difficult offensive skills in hockey. The key to deflecting a moving puck toward the goal is to get in position near the goal (preferably, off to the goalie's side, where you can tip the puck between the goalie and the post) with your legs spread and knees slightly bent for stability. Have your stick on the ice and your weight on the stick. The best chances for tip-ins come on centering passes from teammates and low slap shots from the points and, if your stick is in the air, the puck may be past you before you can make contact with it.

Just as a good football receiver watches the ball into his hands, watch the puck all the way onto your stick blade. The most common fault in deflecting shots is to take your eyes off the puck at the last moment and look to where you want the puck to go. No one has perfect control of a deflection, so in general just try to steer the puck toward an open part of the net. As in any shot, be alert for a rebound.

Deflections.
Deflections can often be converted into scores—if you're properly positioned in front of the net.

SCREENING AND SCREEN SHOTS

Screening the goalie means blocking his vision by standing between him and the puck. It is a legal tactic as long as you don't stand in the crease or block the goaltender's movement. When screening for a teammate, keep your back to the goalie and face the approaching shot. Facing the shot not only gives you an opportunity to try for a deflection, it also reduces your chances of injury because you can see the shot coming and because you have a lot more padding on the front of your body than on the back.

When screening a goalie, expect to take some heavy hits from opposing defensemen—whose job it is to move you out of scoring position—and from the goalie, who will want to get you out of his line of sight. Beware of being goaded into taking a retaliatory penalty.

When you are the shooter who is taking advantage of a screen—one set up either by a teammate or by an opposing defenseman who has backed up on his own goalie—keep your shot low, where it has less chance of hitting the screening player's body and more chance of beating the goalie. You can take further advantage of a screen by shooting "against the grain." For example, suppose you have the puck, the flow of play is from your right to your left and the goalie is moving across the crease in the same direction. If the goalie moves into a screen or is suddenly screened while he's moving, you can beat him by sending your shot from left to right, that is, against the flow or "grain" and back to the point the goalie just left. Not only will you have the screen working for you, but you also will make the goalie's momentum work against him.

Screening the opposing goalie is a legal means of improving your team's scoring chances.

DRILLS

Dry-Land Shooting

The puck-scarred cellar walls and battered garage doors of thousands of North American homes are mute proof that you don't need ice to practice your shot. However, when you work on your shot in your driveway or down in your basement, try to use a slick shooting surface, such as a piece of Formica, linoleum or plastic laminate. These surfaces more closely resemble the slickness of ice than do cement or macadam and thus give you a more realistic feel for the various shots. Also, make sure you always shoot at some sort of target. Don't just blast away haphazardly, developing power at the expense of accuracy. Finally, work on *all* your shots, not just the slap shot and the forehand.

Of course, nothing will duplicate the feel of real ice, and you should get on-ice shooting practice whenever possible, even if it means taking your shots off a small frozen puddle in the schoolyard. If you have some free time at a team practice — and you will if you're one of the first ones on the ice — you can work on your various shots by shooting at the empty nets or against the boards. But, when you shoot, pick a target, even if it's only the place where the blue line is painted on the boards.

A Shooting Board

One of the best targets for shooting practice — on or off the ice — is a shooting board. You can make one by taking a 4-by-6-foot sheet of plywood and cutting out the four corners to a depth and length of about 18 inches. Some coaches also like to make the board slightly less than 6 feet wide so there will be some open space near the posts. Fasten hooks to the board so that it can be hung on the crossbar of the goal. A shooting board will help you improve your accuracy and work on all of your shots, especially the fast-rising shots and hard shots from close range that goalies, understandably, object to facing during practice.

A shooting board.
A homemade shooting board, like the one drawn here, can help you become an extremely accurate shooter.

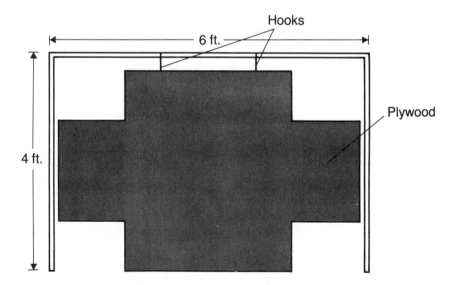

Slap-Shot Drills

The simplest slap-shot drill involves lining up an arc of pucks in front of the goal and shooting them in succession. Work at keeping the shots as low as possible, and on the net.

The Slap/Tip Drill

Since many slap shots are taken from the blueline and are intended to be deflected on goal, it's better to work with teammates in a drill that lets you practice slap shots and deflections. Start this drill with a defenseman on the board-side point (the passer), a defenseman at the middle point (the shooter) and the other players in the corner beside the goalie. A player from the corner passes the puck to the board-side point man and breaks for the goal. The board-side point man passes over to the middle point man, the shooter (much as would happen in a game), and the shooter takes a low slap shot on goal, which the man coming in from the corner tries to deflect in. Repeat the drill until every player has had a chance to tip a shot. Then run the same drill from the other corner so that the passing defenseman will now get a chance to shoot.

The slap-shot drill.
To groove your swing for taking slap shots, simply place several pucks in front of you and take your shots in rapid-fire succession.

Backhand Drills

1. Place a cone or similar marker about 25 feet in front of the goal. As you approach the cone, swing to your backhand side and shoot.

2. Line up the left-hand shooting players on the left side of the rink behind the red line, and the right-hand shooting players on the right side of the rink behind the red line. Station a coach or player in each corner with a supply of pucks. One at a time, players skate into the faceoff circle, take a pass from the corner, pull the puck to their backhand and shoot as they cut across the goal mouth.

Flip-Shot Drills

One of the best ways to work on this shot is to place a bench in front of the goal and snap the puck over it and under the crossbar. The shooting board also comes in handy here, since even a substitute goaltender shouldn't have to submit to lying on the ice while players work on their flip shots, and in a game the flip shot is rarely used against a goalie who is still on his feet.

The Snap-Shot Drill

In this drill, a coach or teammate stands in the corner beside the goalie with a supply of pucks. You skate in on goal through the faceoff circle, take a pass from the corner and *immediately* snap a shot on goal. The idea is to get the shot away quickly and not allow yourself the luxury of drawing the puck back and sweeping it forward as you would in the standard forehand. You can also benefit from doing this as a stationary drill, standing in the slot, taking passes in rapid succession and snapping the shots on goal.

In any drill and in any shooting situation, *Look before you shoot.* And, if you have to choose between power and accuracy, choose accuracy. If you talked to the goalies around the NHL, they would tell you that what separates the great scorers — Gretzky, Brett Hull, Lemieux and others — from the average players is not the overwhelming power of their shots but, rather, a quick release and an instinct for the net.

A quick release means the goalie cannot get set for the shot, so you make up in time what you give up in power. For example, a sudden shot from 30 feet out going 70 mph can have a greater chance of scoring than a 90 mph shot taken from the same place by a player who had to hesitate or wind up, giving the goalie time to come out and cut down the shooting angle.

As for accuracy, it does *not* mean that you have to be able to put the puck

A goal, such as the one being scored here, is hockey's *denouement*—
the sudden untangling of the offensive plot.

through a mailbox slot from 60 feet. What it means is that—even from a long distance or a bad angle—you should at least be able to get your shots on the net consistently. Or, as Mike Bossy once said, "make the goalie make the save." When you
get your shot on net, anything can happen.

A shot, then, is the sudden untangling of the offensive plot. It is the last of
your individual offensive skills. Now it's time to apply these skills—skating, stickhandling, shooting and passing—in the context of a team sport.

5

Offense

Hockey, as the game was originally played on frozen ponds and lakes, was a wide-open, freewheeling sport involving a maximum of skating and stickhandling and, because of the absence of boards, a minimum of body contact. Around the turn of the century, however, as the game was brought indoors – to be corralled first in boarded rinks, later in huge arenas – its character inevitably changed. Less space and the looming presence of the confining (and some might have said "confounded") boards tilted the game clearly toward the defense. Not only could defenders simply force the play to the boards and knock attackers off the puck, but the attacking team was, until the 1920s, handicapped by a rule against forward passing. Only backward and lateral passes were permitted. Forced to try to stickhandle through layers of defenders, individual attackers found themselves quickly stripped of the puck. The forward pass changed that. With the advent of the forward pass the game changed – particularly the concept of attack – from one relying on the soloist, the stickhandling and skating virtuoso, to one that made use of the entire orchestra. The desirability – indeed, the necessity – of advancing the puck by passing it from one player to another – made hockey a game of *team* strategy and tactics. Without the ability to comprehend a system of play and to work within the structure of a team system, offensive and defensive, you cannot regard yourself as a complete hockey player. Let's begin our discussion of team play with a look at offense.

Offense begins not in your attacking zone but at whatever point on the ice your team gets possession of the puck. That usually happens in the defensive zone, which means the foundation of your offense, what gets it under way, is your system for breaking the puck out of your defensive zone and starting a counterattack. You won't score any goals off a breakout play but it *is* the most important play in hockey since your whole offense depends on it.

89

Bobby Orr's speed and ability to rush the puck the length of the ice gave defensemen an offensive role and helped usher hockey into the modern era.

BREAKOUT SYSTEMS

While coaches have designed numerous breakout plays, the breakouts we will consider are basic systems on which almost all breakout plays are based. Their object is to move the puck away from the attackers and to start your team's play toward the opposite goal.

Positioning

A team usually comes into possession of the puck when one of its defensemen gains control of it in the corner. In the diagram below, let's say your team is in its defensive zone and your right defenseman (RD) has the puck in your right corner. The other defenseman (LD in this case) is still protecting the area in front of your goal. In this situation, the puck-side wing (RW in this case), also called the *strong-side wing*, positions himself about halfway down the boards, facing the defenseman who has the puck. The center, who is roughly 30 feet deep in the defensive zone, begins curling toward the RD. The wing on the other side—the left wing (LW), or weak-side wing in this example—is about halfway inside the zone, roughly in the middle of the left lane.

Set-up for a simple breakout play.

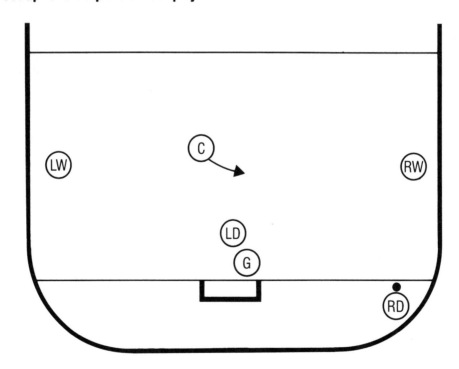

Now, as the RD takes control of the puck, he can initiate one of several plays:

1. *He can rush the puck.* If he has open ice in front of him and *if* he is a superior skater, he can carry the puck out himself. But those are big ifs. Beginning with Bobby Orr of the Boston Bruins in the late 1960s, and continuing with Paul Coffey of the Pittsburgh Penguins in the 1990s, there have always been a few—very few—defensemen with the speed and stickhandling skills to rush the puck themselves. If you are lucky enough to be that much better than the players you are competing against, then by all means take advantage of your talent. However, even then there are rules to consider.

First, your defensive partner must be careful to stay back, coming up ice slowly behind the play in case there is a sudden turnover. The three forwards, reading the defenseman's intent, break up-ice with the play and remain ready for a lead pass. If the defenseman carries the puck all the way into the attacking zone, it's critical that the wing on his side stay back to cover the point—that is, the position on the blue line that the defenseman would normally take. In the diagram below, the RD has rushed the puck deep into the attacking zone and the RW has dropped back to cover.

After taking a shot on goal or after passing to a teammate, the defenseman

Breakout option #1: rushing the puck.

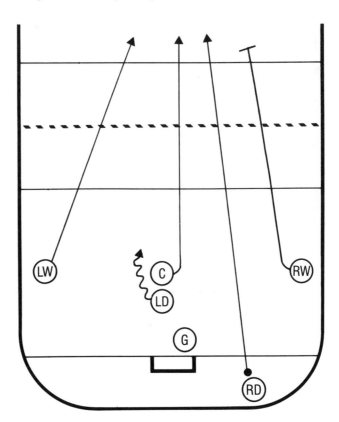

who has rushed the puck should return to his point position as quickly as possible and let the wing who is temporarily covering that position get back into play. More often than not, though, the defenseman gaining possession in the corner will have a forechecker (an opposing forward trying to regain possession of the puck) pressuring him and will not have the luxury of open ice and may not have the ability to make a rush. In this case, there are other options:

2. *The right defenseman can pass the puck to the strong-side wing.* In turn, the wing passes to the center, and as the line moves out of the zone, both defensemen break behind the play.

Breakout option #2: pass to right wing.

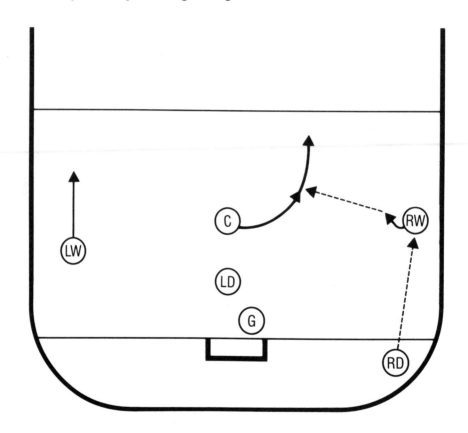

3. *The right defenseman can pass to the weak-side wing.* Here, the pass is sent around the boards to the opposite wing.

Breakout option #3: pass to weakside wing.

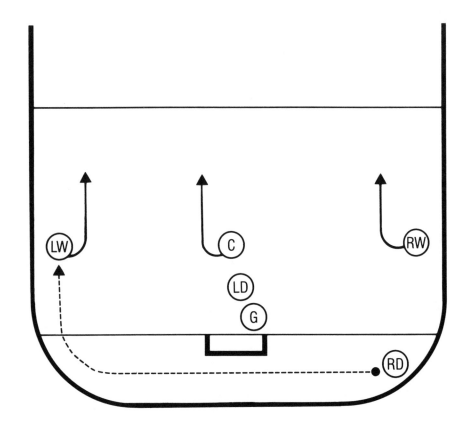

4. *The right defenseman can pass to the center.* This is one of the best options (if the pass route is open) because now your team is breaking up the middle and the center has a choice of passing to either side. In the diagram, the center has passed left.

Breakout option #4: pass to the center.

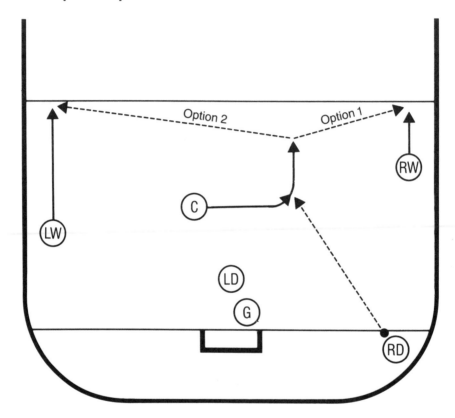

5. *The right defenseman can carry or pass the puck behind the net.* This is one of the most common game situations in scholastic, college and professional ranks in which systematic heavy forechecking—the intense efforts of two or sometimes all three opposing forwards to swarm upon your defensemen in an effort to force them to give up the puck—is the norm. By taking or passing the puck behind the net, the RD uses the goal cage as a kind of safety barrier while he sets up a whole new series of breakout options. These include:

1. *Burning the forechecker.* If the forechecker chases the right defenseman behind the net—a poor play on the forechecker's part—the RD simply skates out in the opposite direction and makes his breakout pass to one of the forwards. In the diagram below, the forechecker comes in from the left only to have the RD escape by skating out to the right.

Burning the forechecker.

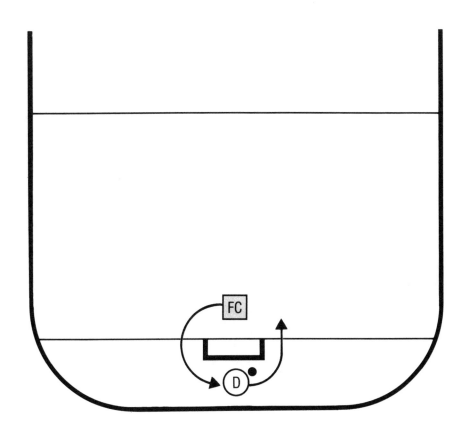

2. *Center swinging behind the net*. If the forechecker stays in front of the cage—as he should—then the center can scoot behind the net, take the puck from the RD and start the breakout.

Center swinging in behind the net.

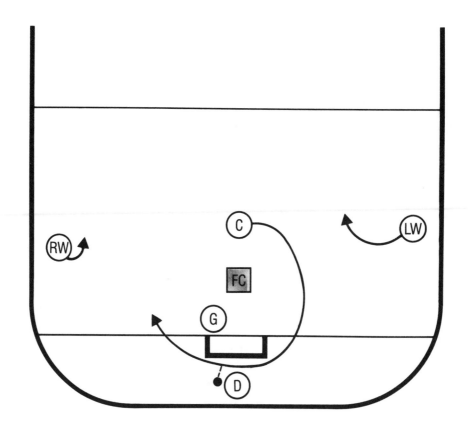

3. *Passing to the defenseman in the corner.* Very often both defensemen are behind the goal line (in which case the center covers the slot). In this instance, let's assume there is forechecking pressure on the right defenseman behind the net but that he is in possession of the puck. In the diagram, we see that the RD's defensive partner, the left defenseman, has left the front of the goal (he should not do this if the opponents have possession) and gone to the corner. Now the RD can pass or even kick the puck over to him and he should be free to pass either to the center or to the strong-side wing, or to give the puck back to the RD. In general, the left defenseman is responsible for the left corner, the right defenseman for the right corner.

Passing to the defenseman in the corner.

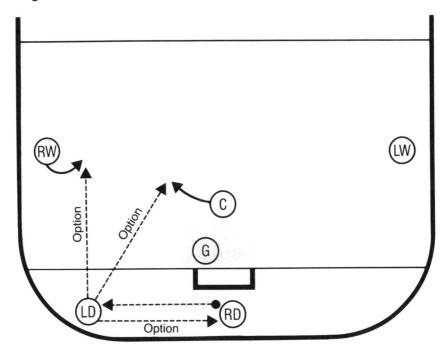

In all of these plays, *beware of making a pass in front of your own net.* You will see it done at the higher levels of hockey, but only when players are 100 percent certain they can complete the pass. At the lower levels of hockey, making a pass in front of your own net is a dangerous play. An errant pass, or even a bad bounce, could lead to an interception in the prime scoring area.

DRILLS FOR BREAKOUT PLAYS

Breakout plays look easy on paper but can be difficult to execute under game conditions because your opponents won't be standing around watching you pass the puck. They're going to be forechecking you. Nevertheless, it's best to practice breakouts without opposition at first, just to acquire a feel for patterns and positioning. Later, you can start practicing these plays against forecheckers.

Your coach can run a breakout drill by assembling one five-man unit at center ice and shooting a puck into your defensive zone where you and your teammates retrieve the puck and start a breakout. To make the drill more interesting each five-man unit should also be allowed to take the puck the length of the ice for a shot on goal.

As you and your teammates learn your responsibilities on breakouts, you can make the drills more difficult — and more realistic — by sending in one, two or three forecheckers, putting pressure on the defenseman who retrieves the puck and reducing his passing options. Such pressure forces him to be quick and decisive in initiating the breakout.

A breakout isn't much fun to watch or to work on, but, as the single most important team play in hockey, it's something your team should work on at every practice.

PLAY IN THE NEUTRAL ZONE

The neutral zone (the area between the blue lines) is the staging ground for your offense and the best part of the ice for making use of the weaving, improvisational play that is increasingly popular in today's game, and is gradually replacing the rigid system of forwards moving through center ice three abreast, each man in a prescribed lane.

When moving into and through neutral ice, one of the first things you want to think of is "head-manning" the puck. "Head-manning" means that the player with the puck passes it ahead to a teammate nearer the attacking blue line. There is a story told in Montreal that when Canadiens' Hall-of-Fame defenseman Doug Harvey would head-man the puck to the legendary Maurice "the Rocket" Richard, it would often be with the admonition, "Here, Richard, now do your job." The implication was that Harvey's "job" was done when the puck came to center ice and that Richard's job, as a forward, was to take over from there and figure out a way to get it into the attacking zone. In today's game, neutral-zone play is everyone's job.

Role of the Defensemen

Defensemen should be quick to head-man the puck to open forwards. But in the modern game, that doesn't always mean passing to the forward who is streaking for the attacking zone. Don't be afraid to pass to a teammate who may be cutting diagonally in front of you, or even to one who is curling back toward you, providing that the player is open and thus is the best target for your pass. Also, whether passing or receiving, defensemen, like all other skaters, should be moving. You're too easy to check when you're standing still.

Defensemen should also be staggered in relation to one another. If your partner is up near the red line with the puck, you should stay slightly behind him, backing him up in case of a turnover. If you happened to be the defenseman carrying the puck into neutral ice on a rush, don't be afraid to circle back into your zone and restart the play if your teammates are covered and you find yourself checked. Surrendering a zone once you obtained it used to be a great taboo in North American hockey. But one of the things North Americans have learned from the European game is that it's often better to circle back, regroup, and *then* make an organized attack, than to try to force a play where the opportunity doesn't exist.

Finally—and here is another departure from traditional practice—*defensemen, don't hesitate to fill one of the forward lanes if it becomes open.* If you stay with the play and move into the attacking zone on the wing, it is up to one of the forwards to read your move and stay back and cover your point.

Role of the Forwards

The fundamental principle of neutral-zone play for forwards is: Maintain width and depth of attack by filling the three lanes and by not skating three abreast. In the more traditional style of hockey, filling the lanes was a simple case of the center taking the middle lane while each of the wings stayed in one of the outside lanes. But today's game encourages more crossing over by the three forwards. Thus, all forwards must learn to watch the movement of their line mates and read a play instantly. If a line mate releases and breaks into your lane, then in most cases, you will want to maintain the width of attack by leaving your lane and filling his.

There are several advantages to these weaving maneuvers. First, lateral movement gives you the freedom to move away from coverage and, thereby, to confuse the defense. Second, it creates better passing angles for both the receiver and the passer. If you haven't already noticed, it is much easier to pass to a teammate who is cutting *across in front of you* than to one who is moving away from

The single crossover.

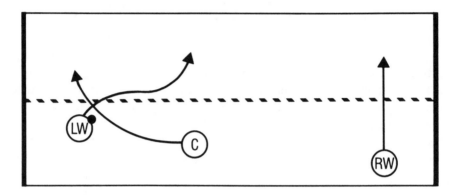

The double crossover.

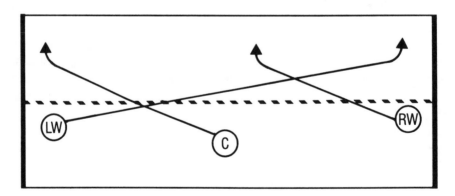

you. Likewise, it is easier to receive a pass coming from your side than one coming up from behind you. Weaving facilitates passing. Furthermore, by passing to a laterally moving player, you reduce the chances of a play going offside. In executing these weaving patterns the general rule is, *break away from the boards toward open ice*, to give yourself more area to work with.

OFFENSIVE-ZONE PLAY

The purpose of all offenses is to create scoring chances by bringing about, then exploiting, a numerical advantage. But before we consider the various options available when a three-man line works against a two-man defense, we should consider the general principles governing team play in the offensive zone.

1. If your play is stopped at the blue line—and if it is not part of your game plan to dump the puck into the zone and chase it—then don't be afraid to pass the puck back to your defensemen, return to neutral ice and reorganize.

2. As you enter the attacking zone, try to move the puck *away* from the flow of the defense. If, for example, you are bringing the puck down the right-wing boards toward the corner and your opponents are beginning to converge on you, then you want to move the puck to a teammate, preferably to the man in the slot or, if that is impossible, to a teammate who is open and will have more time to make a play or take a shot.

3. *Look* before you pass. Too many times a player skating beside or behind the net will pass the puck blindly into the slot in hopes that a teammate is there. The pass usually ends up on the stick of an opposing defenseman: a needless giveaway. Have the courage and confidence to handle the puck responsibly, holding it until you find the open man or until you can take a good shot yourself.

4. *Expect* (don't just hope for) rebounds. Don't go cruising behind the net or turning away from the play after you shoot. Follow up on your shot by charging toward the goal mouth, keeping your stick down and ready for the rebound.

5. One forward should remain "high" in the zone, about halfway to the blue line, ready to backcheck (that is, to skate back up ice in a defensive role) in case your opponents get the puck and break out fast. In the event of a turnover you don't want all three forwards trapped deep in the offensive zone.

6. Defensemen, when shooting from the point, keep your shot low to take advantage of screens and give your teammates the best chance for a tip-in.

7. Remain facing the puck as much as possible.

8. When the three forwards set up in the offensive zone, you should try to maintain a triangle (see diagram). This not only gives your attack depth and width, but also provides support and passing options for the puck carrier. For example:

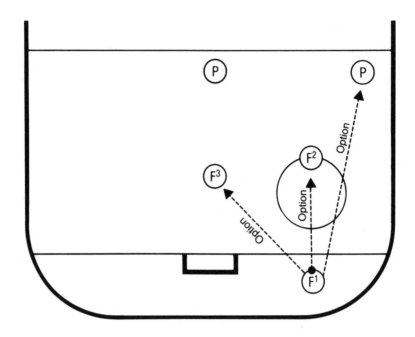

The puck carrier (F¹) in the right corner can pass to: a) the forward (F³) in the slot, b) the other forward (F²) at the top of the circle, or c) to the strong-side defenseman (P).

Or, in this triangular set-up

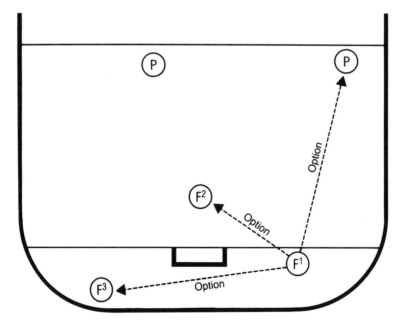

the puck carrier (F^1) can a) pass to F^2 in the slot, b) pass behind the net to F^3 who can then try to pass into the slot or c) go up the boards to the strong-side defenseman. Note, too, that, in both of these situations, the man in the slot is not only in prime shooting position but is also the high man, in good position to back-check and help the defense in case of a turnover.

With the puck at the point, the triangle might look like this:

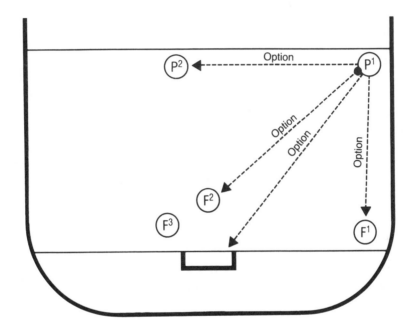

Here, the defenseman with the puck (P^1) can shoot on goal with F^2 in position to screen, and F^3 ready for a deflection or rebound. If no shooting lane is open, the defenseman can pass across to his defensive partner, or, if all else fails, he can pass down the boards to F^1 in the corner.

By the way, we have designated our forwards F^1, F^2 and F^3 rather than C (center), RW (right wing), LW (left wing) because all of the interchanging of positions in the attacking zone (life in the defensive zone is much more disciplined!) makes the old designations seem too restrictive.

MATCHUPS

Having considered the general principles of offensive hockey in each of the three major zones, let's look at some of the specific manpower matchups that are likely to occur in a game.

The Breakaway

This is a relatively rare situation in which you break in alone—usually by receiving or intercepting a pass in neutral ice—with only the goalie to beat. A lot of otherwise great scorers have difficulty on breakaways because the situation gives them too much time to think. Instead of shooting on instinct, as you would in a more familiar game situation, you tend to think too much about the fact that you are in alone and thus think yourself out of a goal, shooting when you should fake, or faking when you should shoot. To simplify the breakaway, follow this rule of thumb: If the goalie comes way out of his net to try to cut down the angle, then you should fake (or "deke") around him. If the goalie stays back in his cage giving you a substantial portion of net to shoot at, take it. Shoot. If you shoot from 15 or 20 feet out, the goaltender probably won't be fast enough to make the save.

What you *don't* want to do is try to pick a small opening on a goaltender who is playing his angles well.

Also, make sure that, as you approach the goal, you have the puck in a shooting position—that is, you are cradling it on the side from which you would take your normal forehand shot rather than carrying it in front of you in what is purely a stickhandling position. A goaltender who spots you approaching the net with the puck out in front of you is either going to poke-check it away (more later) or else go sliding into you, in either case spoiling your breakaway before you even take a shot.

1-on-1

In this situation it's you, the puck carrier, versus one defenseman. Try to get that defenseman to make the first move—which will often turn out to be his first mistake! If the defenseman backs up toward his goalie—say, if he skates across an imaginary line extending across the slot from the middle of the two faceoff circles—then by all means use him as a screen and *shoot low*.

If the defenseman moves *toward* you to try to hit you with a body check, use a stickhandling maneuver to avoid the check and get around the defenseman who,

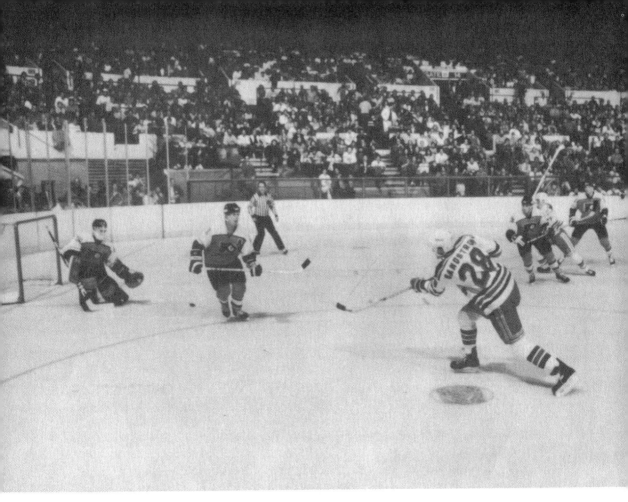

1-on-1.
Here, the forward gets his shot away before the defenseman moves in to fill the shooting lane.

by then, will be leaning in the wrong direction and will most likely be out of the play. You can fake outside and cut inside, fake inside and cut outside, stop (or slow down) and let the defenseman pass in front of you, slip the puck through the defenseman's legs then swing around him to recover the puck or, if you have the ability and speed, speed up and simply outskate the check. Another good trick is the fake shot. Wind up as if you are starting a slap shot and, as the defenseman drops to block the shot (or even if he only stiffens in anticipation), pull the puck back and stickhandle around him.

2-on-1

At the very *least* this situation should result in a good shot on goal.

The keys here are for you, the puck carrier, and your line mate 1) to stay far enough apart so that one defenseman can't cover both of you, and 2) to react to the way the defenseman tries to play the situation.

In carrying the puck down on the defenseman, your first move should be *away* from your line mate. For example, if you are breaking down the right wing with the puck and the center is breaking with you in the middle lane, you want to pull that defenseman covering you over to the board side (your right). Now, as you make your cut to the right, you have to "take a read" on the defenseman. Is he coming over with you or is he hanging back? If he tries to stay in the middle—that is, if he hangs back covering a possible pass—then you'll probably have enough room to skate right by him and go in alone. On the other hand, if the defenseman plays the situation aggressively and comes rushing toward you, then you can pass the puck to your line mate, who should have only the goalie to beat.

A Simple 2-on-1 Drill. Here is a simple, efficient 2-on-1 drill that involves the entire team and makes maximum use of ice time. Start with a goalie in each net, a double line of forwards in the corners at opposite ends of the rink and two groups of defensemen at the red line, one group on either side of the ice (see diagram). The defensemen have the pucks. To start the drill, the first defenseman in line skates forward to the blue line and passes to one of the two forwards in the line facing him. The defenseman then retreats and sets up in position (just as he would in a game) while the two forwards come skating down on him in a 2-on-1. Meanwhile, the same thing is happening at the opposite end of the rink.

After a rush, the forwards go to the end of the opposite line of players and the defenseman goes to the end of the line he just came from. Coaches should switch the groups of forwards to the unused corners and, likewise, have the defensemen swap sides so that all players will gain experience taking and making plays to both their forehands and backhands.

2-on-2

This is a more typical game situation, and whether or not a good scoring chance results depends upon whether you can reduce the 2-on-2 to a 2-on-1, either through your offense's creativity or by a defensive mistake.

Again, the two men on offense must *stay wide*. Staying far apart gives you and your line mate room to work, and at the same time gives the defensemen the maximum area to worry about. If the defensemen stand up at the blue line (taking

A Simple 2-on-1 Drill

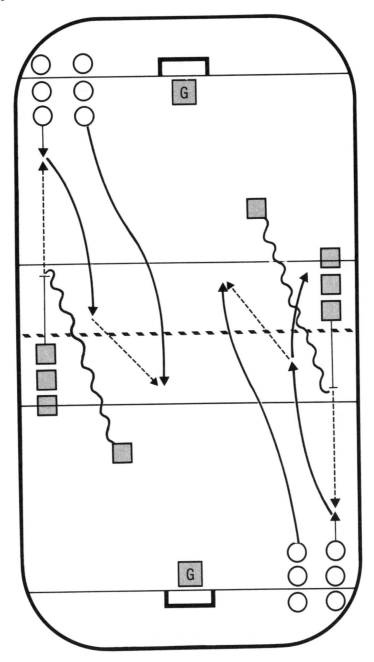

The first defenseman (indicated by a square) in each line skates forward and passes the puck to one of the two forwards (indicated by circles) in the front of their lines. The defenseman then skates backwards toward his goal and defends against the forwards' rush.

away your room for a drop pass) and play you one-on-one, then your best move might be to shoot on net and drive for the rebound or shoot the puck around the boards, whereupon the forward without the puck puts on a burst of speed and tries to beat the defenseman to the puck as it comes around the rink.

If the defensemen back in and give you a little more room to work with, you might be able to fake a rush between them and, as they squeeze in toward you, pass to your uncovered winger for a shot on goal.

A 2-on-2 can also be a good situation for a drop pass (the one exception to the "stay wide" rule.) Here, you cut in front of the defense, drawing one or both defensemen with you, and simply drop the puck for your trailing partner who can then shoot, rush (if he has room) or flip the puck back to you.

To practice the 2-on-2 matchup, use the 2-on-1 drill format, but this time have the defensemen work in pairs.

2-on-1.

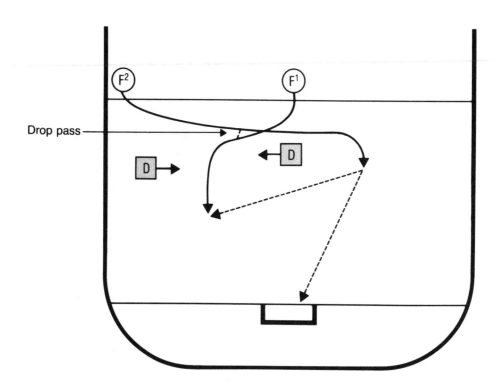

Here we enter into an area where there are limitless variations on what can happen. The situation gets even more complex when you consider that, besides facing two defensemen, one or two of your forwards will probably be covered by (or at least pressured by) backcheckers. So, instead of a long list of what are often complicated and sometimes impractical plays, let's consider some basic plays to use in the most commonly occurring situations.

Dump and Chase. Fans don't like it and neither do some coaches, but if those defensemen are checking you at the blue line ("standing you up" in the vernacular of the game) and if they're getting a lot of help from aggressive backcheckers, you'll find it difficult to pass or carry the puck into the zone. Your best play—like it or not—might be to dump and chase. Here's how it works:

3-on-2: the dump-and-chase.
F³ receives F¹'s carom shot off the boards, and F¹ and F² move in to support.

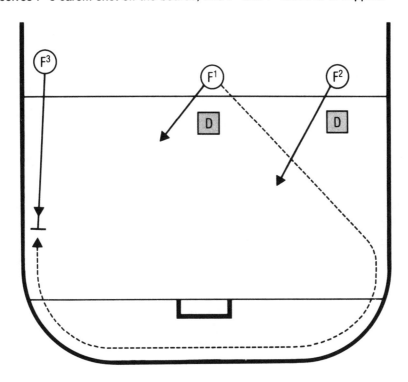

Let's say you're the center (F^1), there's a defenseman in front of you and both your wings are covered (one by a backchecker, one by a defenseman). To break this coverage, you shoot the puck into the corner. That is a signal for the wing on the opposite side (F^3 in this case) to accelerate past his man and try to retrieve the puck as it caroms around the boards. You and the other forward (F^2) then get into support positions, setting up the basic offensive triangle.

Of course, it is better to maintain possession and work the puck into the zone, *provided that* the defense gives you room. Here are some ways to work the puck in:

The Drop Pass. This play isolates one defenseman, reducing the 3-on-2 to the more favorable 2-on-1.

Once the puck is over the blue line, you, the puck carrier, swing wide, drawing a defenseman with you. Your line mate, reading the play, cuts behind you to take the drop pass, exactly as he would in a 2-on-1.

The Puck-Carrier Delay. In this play you carry the puck into the zone down the center lane and right at the two defensemen. Then you suddenly stop. When one of the defensemen recovers and starts rushing toward you, his charge should free up the wing on that side for a pass.

Puck on the Wing. If the puck should enter the attacking zone down one of the wing's lanes rather than in the center lane, the situation becomes easier for the defense since the boards restrict the puck carrier's movement on one side. Here *depth* of attack becomes all-important. As you, the puck carrier, move down the boards, the nearest forward should swing in behind you so that, if all else fails, you can at least pass back up the boards.

If you (F^3 here) can beat the defenseman for either a shot on goal or a pass to F^1, by all means do so. But, if that isn't possible, recognize your option of passing back to F^2 rather than trying to force a play where the opportunity does not really exist.

Puck on the wing.

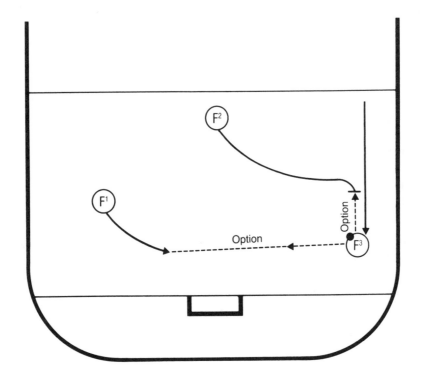

DRILL. Here's a drill where you can use the entire ice surface and work on both your breakout and 3-on-2 line rushes at the same time. Start the drill as you would a breakout drill, with the coach shooting the puck into what would be your defensive zone, the defensemen going in to retrieve it and then playing it up to the forwards for a breakout. The forward line moves down the ice for a shot on goal. But now, instead of ending the drill here, the line comes back up ice, creating a 3-on-2 attack against the two defensemen.

FACEOFFS

A faceoff occurs when an official drops the puck between two opposing players—usually the centers—to start or resume play. Faceoffs are becoming an increasingly important part of the game. In the 1950s a typical NHL game would have about 60 faceoffs. Today that number has risen to 80 or more. The increase is due in large part to the greater number of shots (goalies can and often do hold onto the puck, forcing a faceoff); an increase in goals scored (there is a faceoff at center ice following each goal); and more frequent stoppages caused when players resort to "freezing the puck" along the boards, that is, pressing the puck against the boards with sticks, skates or bodies so that no opponent can gain possession and the play is whistled dead. Every faceoff represents an important chance for your team to gain possession.

The rules require that the two players taking the faceoff be square to each other, facing their opponent's end of the rink and standing approximately one stick's length apart. No other player may be within 15 feet of the two players taking the faceoff until after the puck is dropped. This means that if you are not the player taking the faceoff, you must stand outside of the faceoff circle, which has a 15-foot radius. Players outside the circle must also remain "on-side," that is, may not be positioned ahead of the point where the puck will be dropped.

Before the puck is dropped, the rules require that both players taking part have their stick blades on the ice and that the visiting player put his blade on the ice first.

What normally happens on a faceoff is that the official will hold out the puck, flat-side down; check to make sure that there are no violations (that both sticks are on the ice, that the players taking the faceoff are square to each other, that no other player is in the circle and that all players are on-side), and then quickly drop the puck onto the faceoff dot for the two players to contend for it. Should the official see a violation before dropping the puck, he will warn the offending player. The official will not drop the puck until all players are in proper position. If one of the two players taking the faceoff should commit an infraction and disregard the official's first warning, the official will often send that player out of the circle and insist that one of his teammates take the faceoff instead. This is why, in the late stages of a close game, a team will often have two experienced faceoff men on the ice. Should one get thrown out of the circle, there will be another player experienced enough to take and win the faceoff.

A faceoff is the only set play in hockey and the only time in which your designated forward position (left wing, right wing or center) becomes truly important. Or, as Phil Esposito once jokingly put it, "In hockey you only have a position so you'll know where to line up for the faceoffs."

Preparing to Take The Faceoff

A

B

Keep your bottom hand low on the stick for extra leverage and your eyes on the puck even when it's in the official's hand (A). When the official drops the puck (B), try to be first to scoop it back toward a teammate.

Taking the Faceoff

The center takes the faceoff (which is also referred to as "taking the draw"). If you are a center you should make sure you know where your teammates are positioned (move them if you have to) before you move up to the faceoff dot. As you get set to take the draw, slide your bottom hand down your stick shaft, grabbing your stick just above the blade to give yourself maximum leverage and strength. Watch the puck in the referee's hand so you will know the instant he releases it.

Winning the Draw

Here's a move that will help you win more faceoffs. As the player on the left moves his stick blade toward the puck (A), the player on the right uses his stick to lift his opponent's stick off the ice (B,C). He then scoops the puck back toward one of his teammates (D,E).

A

B

C

D

E

As the official drops the puck you want to scoop it back toward a teammate with a flicking motion of the toe of your blade. A helpful trick here is, first, to push your stick across the faceoff dot, knocking your opponent's stick away and giving yourself the space to make a smooth, uninterrupted draw.

Coaches should keep in mind that centers draw best to their backhand sides. Given the fact that the center is trying to pass the puck to teammates who are positioned *behind* him, it is easier and more natural to do so with a backhand motion than to get the puck on his forehand and turn around. Thus, a coach looking for a shot from the slot on a faceoff in the offensive zone would want a left-shooting center taking the draw from the right side of the goal and a right-shooting center taking the draw from a faceoff that is to the left of the goal.

Here are two plays for offensive zone faceoffs. In this first situation—a faceoff to the right of your opponents' goal—the right wing has moved into a "trigger man" position for a quick shot on goal.

Right side faceoff, right wing as trigger man.

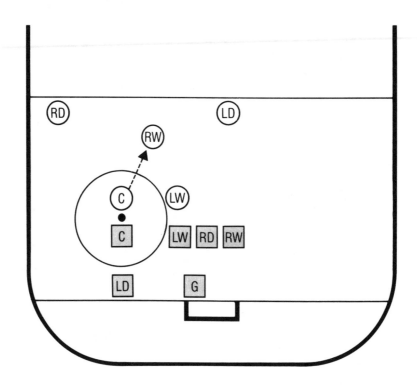

In a more traditional straight-across alignment (one that doesn't leave the right wing's lane wide open as did the previous play) the center can 1) draw the puck back to one of the pointmen, or 2) push the puck over to the board-side wing who can then make a play (probably a pass to the point).

Straight-across faceoff with pass options.

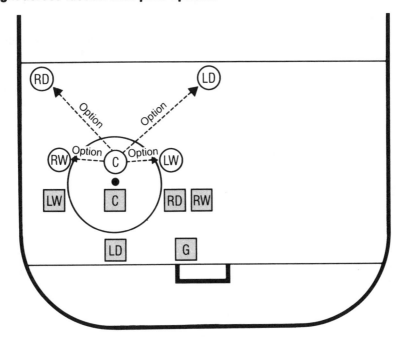

In *any* faceoff situation — offensive, defensive or neutral-zone — there are a few key points to keep in mind, particularly if you are the player taking the draw.

First, know exactly what you want to do if you win the draw. Whom are you trying to pass to? Where is he on the ice? Which side of his body is his stick on? (It is best for the man receiving the puck if you can give it to him on his forehand.) Secondly, make sure your teammates — particularly the player you want to get the puck to — know exactly what you're trying to do. That's why you often see players talking to each other just before a faceoff. Finally, know what you will do if you *lose* the faceoff, which, in the case of the player taking the draw, almost always means checking the opposing center while your teammates get into their offensive or defensive positions, depending on which zone the faceoff is in.

Every faceoff gives you a 50-50 chance of possession. With 80 or more faceoffs per game, winning more than you lose gives your team a big advantage.

POWER PLAYS

Power-play opportunities occur when your opponents have one or two fewer skaters on the ice because of penalties. A good power play will result in a score roughly 20 to 25 percent of the time and will often decide the outcome of the game.

Most coaches have developed their own power-play systems, but the object of all of those schemes is the same—to produce a high-percentage scoring shot by improving the initial 5-on-4 advantage (the typical matchup on power plays) to a 2-on-1. In general they do that either by *overloading* one section of the ice or by *spreading* personnel over a wide area. Let's look at simple examples of each method.

A deep-overload power play.

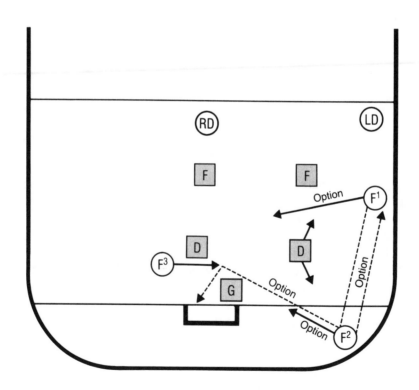

A Deep Overload

In this situation, the three offensive players on the right side (the two forwards and the point man) have created a 3-on-2 since there are only two defenders on that side of the ice. This 3-on-2 further reduces to a 2-on-1 because F^1 and F^2 are working against one defenseman (the low defenseman on the right side). Meanwhile, F^3 occupies the other defenseman in front of the net. Several plays are possible. F^1 and F^2 can trade passes in an effort to tease the defenseman out of position. If the defenseman rushes for F^2, then F^1 breaks for the slot and, unless the defenseman makes an outstanding play, F^2 should be able to pass the puck to F^1 for a shot on goal. On the other hand, if the defenseman gets too close to the forward who does *not* have the puck, then the forward with the puck can simply take a shot on goal. And even if the defenseman manages to keep F^1 and F^2 from shooting or rushing into the slot for a pass, F^3 can always break away suddenly from the defenseman covering him, take a quick pass from F^1 or F^2 and get a shot on goal.

Most power-plays benefit from flopping the wings, that is, putting right-handed shots on the left side and left-handed shots on the right side. Why? Because a right-handed shot shooting from the left wing will have a better angle (that is, a straighter route) to the net than he would if he were on the right wing. Likewise for a left-handed shot on the right wing.

The Umbrella or Spread

The other currently popular power play is the "Umbrella" or "Spread." Strategically, it is the opposite of the overload. In the overload, your team is trying to create a clear advantage by concentrating its force in a small area of ice. In the umbrella, you are creating an advantage by trying to scatter the undermanned defensive team over its entire defensive zone, an area your opponents will often find too big to cover. The umbrella system is popular with teams that have a defenseman (such as the Chicago Black Hawks' Doug Wilson) who is clearly a superior puck handler and has an outstanding shot. That player becomes a lone point man and plays a role much like that of a point guard in basketball.

Here the point man (P) and top two forwards (F¹ and F²) can work against two defenders, possibly getting F¹ or F² free for a shot from one of the circles. F³ and F⁴ occupy the defense down low (that is, deep in the defensive zone) and are free to move to the outside for a pass. The basic idea is to work the puck around the perimeter until someone is free for a shot. The danger here is that if P should give up the puck it may well result in a breakaway and, very possibly, a short-handed goal.

The umbrella power play.

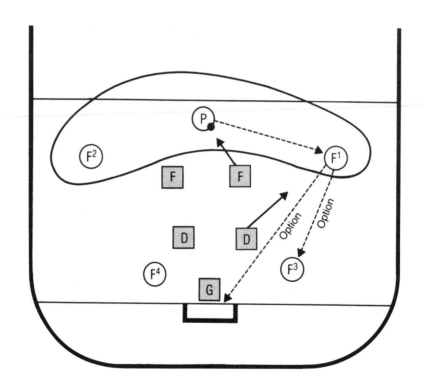

POWER-PLAY DRILLS

Your team can use practice time most efficiently by having the power-play unit work against the penalty-killing unit under game conditions—that is, with a stopwatch and with whistles for all infractions. Since 120 seconds is a long stretch to remain on the ice, particularly in today's up-tempo game, most teams have two complete penalty-killing and power-play units.

TACTICS AND CREATIVITY

If tactics and strategy are important to your offense, so are spontaneity and creativity. An offense that is too predictable is an offense easily defended against. Yet the nature of the game, with its constant swirling action up and down the ice, its sudden changes of personnel, its instant transitions from offense to defense, does not lend itself to the precise, prescribed "X and O" positioning that one finds in football playbooks. Indeed other than the rare penalty shot, the faceoff is the only "set" play in hockey—that is, a play that begins with no player in motion. Everything else happens at top speed. Furthermore, the size of the rink, the noise of the crowd, the fact that players need both hands on their sticks and the speed of the game make it impractical for hockey to use a voice or hand system of signaling, as do baseball, football and basketball teams. Instead, the play you make usually depends on what your teammates do, which, in turn, usually depends on what the defense does.

For example, if you are carrying the puck into the offensive zone and a line mate sees that the area behind you is open, he may move into that area. When he does, you and he know that he expects you to give him a drop pass. You know it because you have done it before and because it will usually result in a shot on goal in that situation. It is a kind of "situational tactic." You give him the puck not because you planned to or because he called for it (though his cutting behind you was a signal of sorts) but because you both know, through experience, that it's a good play to make. Most hockey plays happen in this ad-libbed fashion. Coaches (players, too) would do well to remember that hockey is not, and probably never will be, a game in which you can diagram everything you want to happen and then go out and *make* it happen simply by superior execution. Much of any team's offense depends not so much on that kind of rote learning as on creative, quick-thinking, opportunistic players who, knowing *many* plays and principles, will instantly apply the best ones for any given situation. Obviously, the

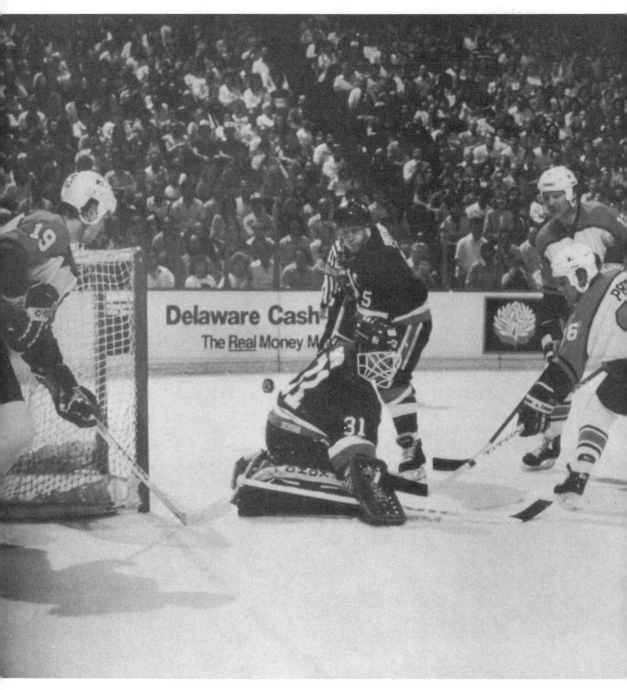

Offense is for opportunists. Note how the offensive man on the left has positioned himself for the possible rebound.

more players play together the better they will learn to know and, more important, to anticipate, each other's moves. That is a good argument for keeping forward lines and defensive tandems together as much as possible. In fact, many European teams regard a three-player line and two-player defensive pairing as a single unit and try to have the same five players on the ice together. (In North America, the tendency is to give forwards slightly shorter shifts than defensemen, so the five-player unit becomes impractical.)

Beyond the intangibles of teamwork, there are a few principles that will help make you a better offensive *team* player and are at least as important as any knowledge of Xs and Os.

1. *Share the puck.* Everyone wants to score goals. But don't let your desire to score tempt you into taking low percentage shots or trying to force an opening for a shot. If a teammate is in a better position to shoot or to advance the play, give him the puck. Being a puck hog is not only a poor tactic, it is demoralizing to a team.

2. *Accept the responsibility of the puck.* When you have the puck you have the responsibility to do something productive with it—shoot, pass or stickhandle. What you don't want to do is to give the puck away. Some players, unwilling to accept the pressure that comes with having possession of the puck, fall into a bad habit of what coaches call "hitting and hoping," that is, passing the puck without looking for a specific target, or simply passing it out in front of the net and hoping a teammate will get to it before the opposing goalie or defenseman does. When you have the puck: Look, decide what you're going to do and make your best effort to do it.

3. *Maintain vision of play.* Again, this means observing the most important rule in hockey: Keep your head up. Know where your teammates are and where the defense is. Don't stare down at the puck.

4. *Play without the puck.* When you do not have the puck you still have a responsibility to the teammate who does. That responsibility is to support him—to get open for a pass, to draw a defender out of the play, to screen the goalie. Play as hard without the puck as you do with it.

5. *Take a check to make a play.* No player likes to get hit. But sometimes it is necessary that you accept a good, hard body check to maintain your concentration and make a good pass to a teammate who may be moving into position to score.

Of course, while your team is out trying to score goals, there are six players trying equally hard to stop you. Which brings us to what many coaches consider the first determinant of winning hockey—defense.

6

Defense

Though hockey is getting more creative and offense-minded — witness the rise in average goals per game in the NHL from 5.9 in 1965-1966 to 7.9 in 1985-86 — the old adage remains true: While offense wins games, defense wins championships.

Most coaches put so much stress on defensive-zone responsibility that you hear even NHL coaches telling their players, "In the offensive zone you can play *your* way, but in the defensive zone you play *my* way."

Even though your team has two players called "defensemen" on the ice, defense is *every* player's job, and it begins the *instant* your team loses the puck. In examining the defensive part of the game let's first consider the individual skills you need to play good defense and then look at some of the most commonly used team systems.

INDIVIDUAL DEFENSIVE SKILLS
FOR ALL PLAYERS

In hockey, the word "checking" refers to the act of impeding the progress of a player with the puck, either by blocking his progress with your body ("body checking") or with your stick (stick checking). Forechecking, which can be done with the stick or the body, refers to the act of checking your opponent in his defensive (your offensive) zone in an effort to regain the puck and continue your attack.

Defense isn't the prettiest part of the game but the goal you prevent is just as important as the goal you score.

Forechecking

Forechecking is your team's first line of defense. It begins as soon as your opponent gains possession of the puck in your offensive zone. Forechecking requires excellent skating, good stick work and a willingness to play the body. (We will discuss body checking separately, later in this chapter.) For now, let's look at the three fundamental stick checking moves—the *poke check*, the *sweep check* and the *stick lift*—and at some of the more common forechecking situations.

The Poke Check

As its name implies, this is a move in which you poke or jab at your opponent's stick in an effort to steal the puck or, failing that, to disrupt your opponent's stick-handling and retard his progress. For maximum range, take your bottom hand off your stick to allow full extension of your top hand as you reach for the puck.

The Sweep Check

This technique is becoming a lost art yet it remains an effective way to steal the puck and to disrupt the puck carrier because it gives you full use of the shaft of your stick instead of only the blade.

You execute a sweep check by putting your stick on the ice and, with only your top hand holding the stick, sweeping it along the ice toward the puck. Bend your knees, get down low and make sure your stick shaft is in contact with the ice, so the puck carrier cannot slide a pass under your stick. As you attempt the sweep check try to turn in the same direction as the puck carrier so that, even if the check is unsuccessful, you will at least be facing the direction of the play, ready to backcheck (more on backchecking in a moment).

The Poke Check

As the name implies, this is a move where you poke at your opponent's stick in order to knock the puck away. Here, the poke checker (the player on the right) suddenly lunges out with his stick, poking the puck away from the puck carrier. Note that the checker has only his top hand on his stick for maximum range.

A

B

C

The Sweep Check

This move takes full advantage of the long shaft of your stick. Here, the checker (on right) not only knocks the puck off his opponent's stick but also gains possession.

A

B

C

The Stick Lift

As the name implies, this is simply the act of putting your stick under your opponent's stick in an effort to lift his stick off the puck. A good stick checker can not only lift his opponent's stick off the ice but also steal the puck with a quick downward and sideways movement.

Maintaining the Angle

The first principle of effective forechecking is to avoid committing yourself so thoroughly that you get trapped up ice while your opponents break out of their zone with at least a momentary manpower advantage. Instead, you should forecheck in such a way that you are *always turning to go in the same direction as the puck carrier*. That is especially true when the puck carrier is holding the puck behind the net—in effect, almost daring you to race in and try to steal it. Don't. Stay about 15 feet in front of the net and wait for the puck carrier to make his move. (If you get impatient and go charging around one side of the net, chances are the puck carrier will skate out the opposite side, leaving you behind the play and feeling more than a little foolish.) When the puck carrier makes his move to

Forechecking the puck carrier. When forechecking a puck carrier who has taken refuge behind the goal, WAIT! If you go around one side of the goal, the puck carrier will escape via the other side. Let your opponent make the first move, then go after him.

130 skate out, you can make your move toward him, but do so at an angle. Your approach should look like this:

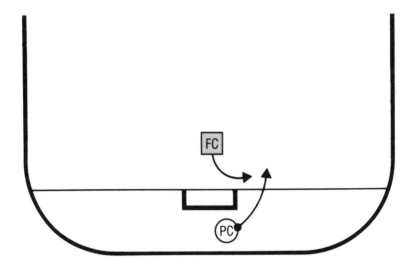

Not this:

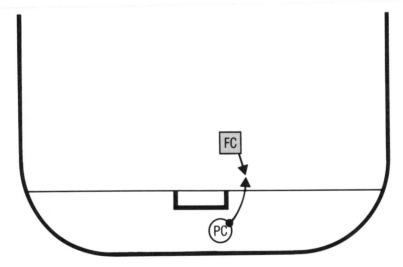

Force the puck carrier toward the boards whenever you can. Not only does that restrict his movement, it also increases the urgency he feels about getting rid of the puck. Under such pressure, he just might make a bad pass.

Forechecking

Note that the forechecker (on right) does not dash straight ahead at the puck carrier, but instead approaches him at an angle (A), thus driving him toward the boards (B). There, the checker succeeds in stealing the puck (C).

A

B

C

A FORECHECKING DRILL

Place half of the defensemen in one corner of the rink and half in a corner at the opposite end of the rink. Give each defenseman a puck. Divide the forwards into two groups, each waiting about 40 feet in front of a goal. A defenseman with the puck carries it behind the net while one of the forwards moves in to forecheck him. Coaches should let the play continue for a few seconds until the forechecker 1) steals the puck or, 2) ties up the puck carrier for what would be a faceoff, or 3) the puck carrier avoids the forechecker and begins a rush up ice.

A forechecking drill.

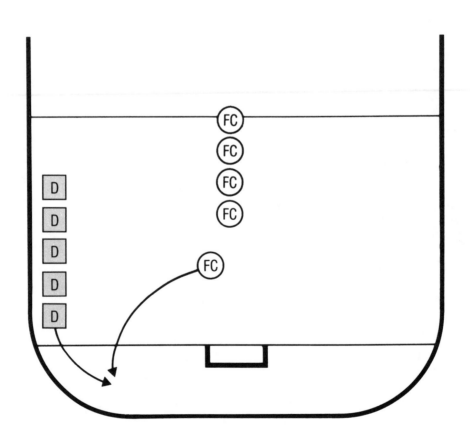

FORECHECKING SYSTEMS

A coach has a choice of sending in one, two or even three forwards to forecheck. But committing all three forwards to forechecking roles is very rare and is apt to be done only by a team that is trailing in the late stages of a game. The rest of the time, coaches will use either a single or a double forechecking system.

Single Forechecker

This is a conservative system, which might be used by a team protecting a lead. One of your forwards, usually the player nearest the puck—though some coaches specify that it be the center—goes in to do the forechecking while the other two forwards start back and cover the opponent's wings. The drawback to this system is that if the forechecker comes up with the puck he may not have a teammate nearby to pass to unless one of the other forecheckers reacts very quickly and gets back into the play. The advantage of this system is that, with only one forward forechecking, the other two forwards can help hamper the opponents' breakout play by providing tight coverage of the wings. Even if your opponents do succeed in breaking out, the single-forechecker system means that there are two forwards backchecking, making this a defense-oriented system.

Double Forechecker

If your team is the type that likes to forecheck aggressively, or if you are trailing late in a game and must press for a goal, you may want to try a double-forechecker system. Here, two forwards go after the puck carrier, the first very aggressively, trying to bump the puck carrier off the puck or trap him on the boards, the second more cautiously, ready to scoop up a loose puck. In effect, the first man plays the body while the second man plays the puck. The disadvantage of this system is simple. If your opponents do succeed in breaking out, you may be left with two forwards stuck deep in the attacking zone. On those rare occasions when all three forwards forecheck, two men should check the puck carrier while the third man stays close by, ready to get any loose puck.

BACKCHECKING

Backchecking means skating back up ice toward your goal line while covering an attacker. It is usually a function of the three forwards since, when the puck changes hands, your defensemen are already backing up and getting into position.

134　Hockey has no greater test of your heart and intensity than your willingness to backcheck, particularly at the end of a sustained attack when the other team has suddenly come up with the puck and you are feeling exhausted. Backchecking is so demanding that old time hockey players used to have a poem about it:

When I was young and in my prime
I used to backcheck all the time.
But now that I am old and gray,
I only backcheck once a day.

The key to effective backchecking is to skate full speed to cover your man the instant your team loses the puck. Generally, wings backcheck on wings—that is your right wing will be coming back with your opponents' left wing and vice

Proper Backchecking Angle

Here, the backchecker (on left) has perfect position: about a half stride ahead of his "check" (opponent), and in between his check and the puck. In effect, the backchecker has isolated his check from the play.

versa. The idea is to pick up your check—that is, the wing you are covering—deep in his own zone so that he will not be an outlet for a breakout pass. If your opponents do succeed in breaking out and the play moves up ice, stay with your check all the way into the defensive zone. The attacking team will often try to throw the backcheckers off by crisscrossing forwards. The rule of thumb here is: *Don't chase crisscrossing attackers*. Instead, simply pick up the player who is coming into your lane. Another general principle is that the backcheckers cover the open forwards and leave the puck carrier to the defensemen.

In backchecking, try to maintain position between your man and the puck so that you will be in good position to intercept a pass. If possible, stay a half-stride ahead of your check—that margin will help you should your check suddenly try to break away from you with a burst of speed. You should also stay as close to your man as possible, thereby giving him little room to work with even if he does get the puck. And, at all times, when you're in doubt about whether to forecheck or backcheck—BACKCHECK.

A BACKCHECKING DRILL

The most realistic backchecking drill is a modification of the 3-on-2 line rush in which the attacking line, instead of having only the two defensemen to beat, must also contend with one or two designated backcheckers. If the drill is run with two backcheckers, one should take each wing. If you do your job properly, the center will have no one to pass to and will have to try either beating the defensemen himself or else dumping the puck into the offensive zone, in effect putting it up for grabs. A 3-on-2 with backcheckers is really a 3-on-4 with the odds in favor of the defense.

TECHNIQUES OF THE DEFENSEMAN

No matter how aggressively your team forechecks or how persistently it backchecks there will be times when your opponents break through these first and second lines of defense. When that happens, it is up to the defensemen to thwart the attack and turn the flow of play around.

In Chapter Two we discussed backward skating, which, if you are a defenseman, is your most important skill. The ability to make accurate passes and the coolness to quarterback the breakout play are also important. After that, checking—stick checking and body checking—is the defenseman's most important asset. We have already looked at the various forms of stick checks. Now let's consider the different types of body checks and the techniques for delivering them.

Body Checking

Knowing when to body-check is as important as knowing how. Remember, when you use your body to stop an opponent you also take yourself out of the play, at least momentarily. And, if you *miss* an attempted check, you will most likely find yourself *completely* out of the play, giving your opponents a brief manpower advantage. (Indeed, by the time you recover, the puck may already be in your net!) Thus, rule one in body checking is that *you must be almost 100 percent certain that you can make the check*. If you're not sure, *don't try it*.

Once you've made up your mind to attempt a body check, don't go lunging out at the puck carrier. That only telegraphs your intention. Instead, wait for the puck carrier to start his move, and make sure he is within roughly a stick's length of you, before you make your move to hit him.

The best time to use a body check is when the puck carrier has made the mistake of dropping his head or when he is trapped between you and the boards with little room to escape. Open-ice body checks on good-skating opponents who have their heads up are rare masterpieces of good timing and technique, spectacular when they work, often disastrous when they fail.

While we have already been through the catalog of penalties, it is worth a reminder that, when body checking, don't take more than two strides toward your opponent (or else it's charging), keep your stick and elbows down (to avoid calls for high sticking or elbowing) and don't stick your leg out to reach an opponent. A leg check will probably get you a two-minute penalty for tripping. Now let's consider the two main types of legal checks.

The Shoulder Check

This is the most common and probably the most effective type of body check. To deliver it you need a good base of support so keep your knees bent and your feet apart and firmly planted on the ice. Like a football tackler, you should look at your opponent's chest, to avoid susceptibility to head fakes and tricky stick-handling.

The shoulder check.
Aim your shoulder at
your opponent's
chest, and, to avoid a
penalty, keep your
elbows *down*.

Deliver the check with the shoulder nearest your opponent. Aim it at the center of his chest, pushing him off the puck. A puck carrier who sees a check coming, even though he can't avoid it, may instinctively bring his stick up to try to cushion the expected blow. Since, in most cases, your opponent will not actually be striking at you, you can easily fend off his stick by pushing it away with your glove or by simply absorbing what should only be a slight push on another part of your well-padded body. If the checked player *does* lift his stick in a threatening manner or puts both hands on it in an effort to shove you away, he should be penalized for high-sticking or cross-checking. By keeping your stick down and by not retaliating, you will avoid matching penalties (a situation in which both players are penalized and, therefore, neither team gets a man advantage) and will have helped your team gain a power play opportunity.

Once you've completed the check, don't stand there admiring your handiwork, leaning on your victim, or letting your opponent hold you, thereby taking you out of the play. Get back into play.

The Hip Check

The hip check is the most spectacular defensive play in hockey, particularly when it is delivered in open ice and the puck carrier (who at the moment of impact will be the *former* puck carrier) goes somersaulting through the air. On the other hand, it's also a high-risk check because, if it fails, you'll be left behind the play and bent over sideways—a poor position in which to skate.

In executing the hip check, you must first bend at the waist so that your chest is facing down at the ice and you are standing sideways in the puck carrier's path. Drive off the leg farther from the puck carrier, aiming your hip or buttocks at his mid-section. Even if you make only slight contact, it will probably be enough to knock the puck carrier off-stride and force him to lose the puck.

The key here is to *move quickly*. A perfect hip check is less a case of your

The Hip Check

The player throwing the hip check has waited until the last moment before bending deeply and throwing his hip into the puck carrier's path (A). The puck carrier, taken by surprise, has neither time nor space to avoid the check and slams into the checker (B). At that moment of contact, the checker's feet are spread apart and planted firmly on the ice for stability (C).

A

skating into your opponent than of your timing your move so perfectly that he cannot help but slam into you.

A final word of caution on all body checking: Don't try it when you are the last man back because, if you fail, the puck carrier will have a breakaway.

Shot Blocking

Shot blocking is a dangerous business, not only because it means you will be hit with the puck from close range, but also because by getting into position to block a shot you are moving into your goalie's line of vision. If you fail to block the shot, your goalie may not see the puck until it is too late.

Courage, timing and position are the three elements of shot blocking. "Guys

B

C

who blocks shots must have bad reflexes," joked one NHL coach in response to a question about the courage it takes to step in the path of a hard shot. But timidity leads to hesitation and there can be no hesitation in shot blocking. Either do it, or get out of the way and let your goalie do it.

Some players block shots by dropping to one or both knees and taking the puck in the midsection or chest. The *kneeling position*, offers the advantage of quick recovery if you miss the puck or if it rebounds off your body, requiring you to scramble back into play. But, as shots get harder and players become more agile skaters able to recover quickly even from a prone position, the *sliding stacked-pad save* seems to be gaining in popularity. Here, you slide — goalie-fashion (more later) — down and *toward* your opponent, keeping one leg on top of the other and taking the shot in your shin pads. This technique is frequently used by wingers who are covering the points.

Positioning is crucial in both the kneeling and sliding techniques. Be within about a stick's length of the shooter before you drop. Make your move when the shooter is committed to the shot. A slap shot is easiest to block since the shooter will telegraph his move with a big backswing and is usually staring down at the puck as he shoots. In this case, try to time your move so that you catch the shooter just as he starts his downswing. If you drop too soon, it's easy for the shooter to fake the shot and stickhandle around you for a closer shot or more dangerous pass.

After you've blocked the shot, scramble back to your feet as quickly as possible. Before getting into the habit of blocking shots you should talk to your goaltender. There may be situations in which your goalie would rather have you concede a long shot than try to block the shot and perhaps create a screen or a deflection.

Shot-Blocking Drills. Other than using lightweight pucks (which don't simulate the action of a real puck) there is no drill for blocking shots that is not unreasonably dangerous. This skill requires timing that can be learned only under game conditions. Scrimmages remain the most realistic opportunities to practice shot blocking before you attempt to block shots in a game.

Shot-Blocking Positions

The standing-position shot block.
Face the puck squarely and keep your stick close to your body (an extended stick is apt to deflect the puck past you and toward your surprised goalie). Use this move only when you're far enough away from your goal so that, if you fail to block the shot, your goalie will still have time to see the puck and react to it.

The kneeling-position shot block.
If you kneel to block a shot, touch one knee to the ice and keep most of your weight on your other leg so that you can get back on your feet quickly.

Shot Blocking Positions (Cont.)

A

B

The sliding stacked-pad shot block.
This is a useful move for stopping a low slapshot from the point. Surprise is important here, so get to the ice quickly (A), and for safety's sake, try to take the shot on your leg pads (B).

A defenseman is always looking at trouble. How well you manage that trouble—breaking up your opponents' plays and helping your team regain possession—depends on your knowing which techniques to use in which manpower situations. Here are some commonly occurring game confrontations and the proper way to play them.

1-on-1

As the puck carrier moves toward you, skate backwards on a slight angle toward your goal, taking away the inside route and influencing the puck carrier to try to beat you on the board side. Don't go rushing toward the attacker unless you are 100 percent sure you can beat him to the puck. Instead, wait for the puck carrier to make his move and then move into him. For example, if the attacker takes what you give him and goes to the outside, force him into the boards and toward the corner, reducing his shooting angle and playmaking space. If the puck carrier tries to beat you to the inside, he will probably be carrying the puck on his backhand (that is, a left-shooting left wing cutting toward the center lane will have to shift the puck to his right side). *Keep him on his backhand* by moving into him. If he comes down the center lane and has time to switch the puck back to his forehand, there's an excellent chance he'll score.

The main rule here is: Play the man, not the puck. If you look at the puck you will be vulnerable to fakes. So look at your opponent's chest and don't be distracted by tricky stickhandling.

DRILL: The basic 1-on-1 drill for forwards is equally useful for defensemen. For valuable extra practice playing the body, try skating through this drill without your stick.

2-on-1

This is a difficult situation but try to remember that time is your biggest asset. Obviously, you don't want to go rushing out at either player—if you rush the puck carrier, he'll pass off; if you rush the open man, you're conceding a shot. The best thing to do is back up, staying between the two attackers and slightly more toward the puck carrier, but never turning your back on the open man. The closer the puck carrier gets to the goal line, the more pressure there is on him to shoot or make a play. If you've maintained proper position you will have cut off the passing lane, forcing the puck carrier to shoot from a bad angle. If the puck carrier tries to pass, you have a chance to intercept or deflect the puck. Even if the pass beats you, there is still the possibility that the other forward will not be able to handle

2-on-1

Here, the defenseman plays the situation perfectly, staying between the two attackers (A) and neither allowing the puck carrier to cut in toward the slot, nor turning his back on the player without the puck. When the puck carrier finally tries to pass (B), the defenseman is in perfect position to intercept (C,D).

A

B

C

D

it and get off a shot. Also, the longer you can delay the play, the greater the chance that a backchecker or your defensive partner will get back in the play and help you.

DRILL: Use the 2-on-1 drill for forwards, with pairs of attackers coming out of both corners so that your team is using the entire ice surface and there are fewer players standing around.

2-on-2

This should be a relatively safe situation. Use man-to-man coverage. If you are the defenseman facing the puck carrier, ride him to the outside just as you would in a 1-on-1. If you are the other (that is, weak-side) defenseman, stay with the open man in case the puck carrier decides to pass. The biggest danger here lies in getting mixed up on a crisscross. Never chase crisscrossing forwards; simply stay where you are and pick up the man skating into your zone.

DRILL: Forwards pair off (a left shot with a right shot) and defensemen pair off in the same combinations you would use in a game. The coach should see to it that the forwards try different plays—drop passes, lateral passes and crossing patterns—to help the defensemen get the most out of the drill.

3-on-2

Retreat. As with the 2-on-1, you want to delay the offense as much as possible until a backchecker can get into the play and turn this into an even-strength situation.

You and your partner should be slightly staggered, with the defenseman nearest the puck playing slightly ahead of the other defenseman. The weak-side defenseman must be ready to react to a pass or to turn and clear a rebound. If the play goes to the corner, one defenseman has to go with it while the other covers the forward most dangerous to the goalie, even though this means letting the third man go. Rarely, however, does a play get this far before a backchecker has arrived to help.

DRILL: You can combine 3-on-2 situations with your standard team breakout drill as described in Chapter Five.

3-on-1

This is real trouble. There is no way to prevent a shot in this situation. About all you can do is stay in the middle of the ice, keep the attack in front of you, retreat and hope your defensive partner or a backchecker will arrive in time to help. If you see a backchecker closing in on one of the forwards, then you can adjust your position, still playing nearest the puck carrier but cheating a bit toward the attacker who does not have a backchecker closing on him. This is not the time to leave your feet to block a shot or to try a body check. If the attackers shoot, pivot instantly and head for the goal, where you might be able to beat them to the rebound.

DEFENSIVE-ZONE COVERAGE

As hockey offenses come to involve more motion and weaving, defenses are changing, too, moving from the man-to-man concept to more zone responsibilities.

Two of the more traditional and fairly simple defensive systems are:

Wings Cover Points and Center Takes High Forward. Here, the strong-side defenseman takes the puck carrier, the weak-side defenseman covers in front of the net, the center picks up the third forward (often in the high slot) and the two wings cover the opponents' points. On the ice, it might look like this:

Wings cover points, center takes high forward.

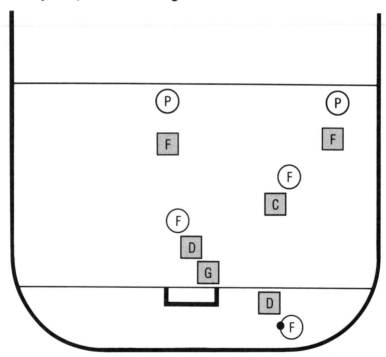

Wings in Deep, Center Stays High. In this system the backchecking wings stay with the opponents' wings deep into the offensive zone while the center stays back and tries to cover both points.

Those are easy systems for youth-level teams. As you progress in hockey, however, you will probably find yourself playing more sophisticated systems in which the forward's role depends not on whether you are left wing, right wing or center, but on whether you are strong side or weak side and whether you are the first, second or third man back into the defensive zone. Coaches are apt to have their own refinements to any system. But here is one popular defensive zone system with position-by-position responsibilities.

The Strong-Side Defenseman

It is up to you to play the puck carrier and force him to the boards. Stay between your opponent and the goal, and by all means play the body. As you force the puck carrier, you should get help from the backchecking forward (also called the low forward). Usually, you will play the puck carrier's body and the low forward will try to strip away the puck. But, if the low forward is closer to the puck carrier, let him take the body and you go for the puck.

The Weak-Side Defenseman

Your main responsibility is coverage in front of the net, where you will be man-to-man with the opposing forward who represents the biggest threat to your goalie. Stay between the player you are covering and the goal and *maintain contact*, either with your body or with your stick, so that your man doesn't slip away from you and get free for a pass. At the same time, *you must always know where the puck is*, and so you must resist the impulse to turn your back on the play and cover your man face-to-face.

The Low Forward

This is the first man back into the defensive zone on the puck side and may be either a wing or the center. If you are the low forward, your job is to help the strong-side defenseman by creating a 2-on-1 on the puck carrier.

The Second Forward (The High Forward, Strong Side)

Like the low forward, the second forward may be either a center or a wing. For example, if your opponents are coming down their left wing and your right wing is the low forward, then your center will be the second forward. Under no circumstances should the weak-side wing (your left wing in this example) come all the way across the ice to act as the high man on the strong side. As second forward, you should be free to come in as low as the faceoff dot, where you can support the strong-side defenseman and low forward and, at the same time, cut off the passing lane to the middle point. If a pass goes to the board-side point, you should still have time to come out at the shooter before he can move into a more dangerous position in the slot.

One type of defensive-zone coverage.

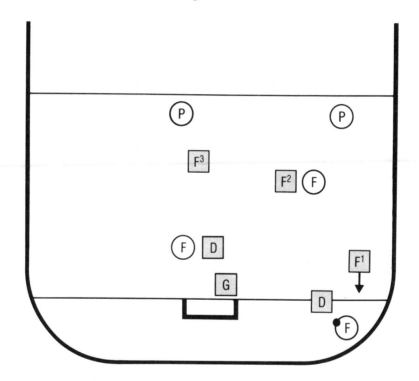

The Weak-Side Forward

You have responsibility for the high slot and, secondarily, for the middle point. But when the puck goes into the corner on your side of the rink, then you become the low forward and move in deep to help the defenseman on your side.

A game situation in which this defense is being used might look like this:

When the puck moves from one corner to the other, the weak-side forward (F³) and weak-side defenseman (D²) must move in quickly to take on the puck carrier and thus become "strong-side" players.

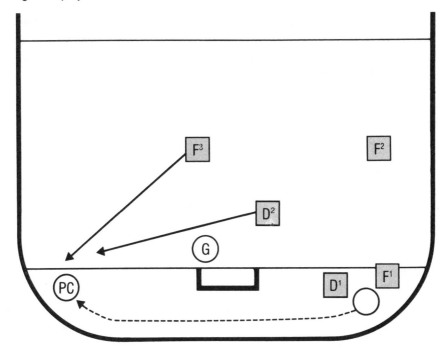

PENALTY-KILLING

There will be times in nearly every game when your team will have to play short-handed, that is, at less than the numerical strength of the other team, because you will be without the services of a player or players penalized for one of the infractions we discussed in Chapter One. Most penalties are for two minutes. If the opposing team scores before the penalty expires, however, the penalized player is allowed to return to play and your team may play at full strength. In the case of a five-minute "major" penalty (usually called for fighting, intent to injure, spearing or drawing blood), the penalized player must remain in the penalty box for the full five minutes, no matter how many goals the opponents might score.

How well your team kills penalties—just as how well it plays when it has the man advantage—will be an important determinant of how frequently it wins. For example, a team that scores on 25 percent of its power plays (considered a good percentage at all levels of hockey) and is scored against only 15 percent of the times it is short-handed (also a good percentage) enjoys a 10 percent advantage over its opponents in the course of a season, if it draws penalties at an average rate. Thus, killing a penalty, while not as much fun as being on a power play, is just as important.

Any time your team must play short-handed, each player's orientation must become defensive. Short-handed goals are a rarity, and the job of the penalty-killers is not to try to score them but to hold the other team off the scoreboard until the penalty expires and the teams are at even strength.

5-on-4

This is the most common penalty-killing situation and one in which a good penalty-killing unit will be successful about 80 to 85 percent of the time. As in all other facets of the game, individual coaches will have their particular refinements, but here are general tactics common to most penalty-killing situations.

Good penalty-killing teams don't wait for the power-play unit to set up. Instead, they start their penalty-killing in their offensive zone. The strong-side forward goes in as a forechecker, approaching the puck carrier at a controlled pace and always ready to swing back out of the zone should his opponents get past him. The weak-side forward stays back, ready to backcheck on the nearest wing when the opposition breaks out. Some coaches may choose a more conservative system in which neither forward forechecks, but instead, both backcheck on the opposing wings so that the center will have no one to pass to and will be forced to dump the puck into the zone.

As your opponents' power play moves through center ice, your defense should stand up at the blue line and try to force the attackers to shoot (rather than carry) the puck into your zone, in which case possession is simply a matter of who wins the race to the puck. If you gain possession of the puck in your defensive zone, remember that you can ice it (that is, shoot it the length of the ice) without the penalty of a faceoff in your zone. When icing the puck, look for the largest hole (that is, the gap between the players ahead of you) and fire the puck through that hole and out of the zone.

The Box Defense. When your opponents do manage to get set up in your zone, it's time for your team to go into a box defense with your four players in a square formation. The two defensemen form the bottom of the box and the two forwards the top. With the puck in the right corner, a typical box defense would look like this:

The box defense.

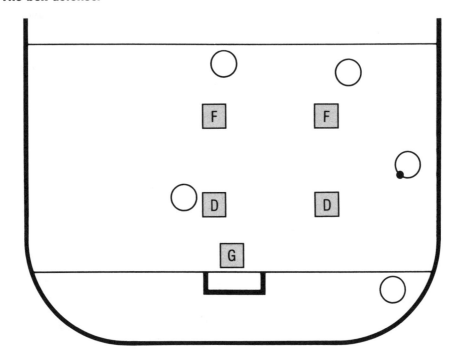

Here, the strong-side defenseman confronts the puck carrier, the weak-side defenseman covers in front of the net and the two forwards cover the point, with the weak-side forward having the option of coming down and taking anyone moving into the high slot.

Patience and restraint are the keys here. Leave your position in the box *only* when you know you have an excellent chance to get the puck; otherwise, stay in the box, forcing your opponents to pass around the perimeter and take low-percentage shots from the outside.

5-on-3

You have much less chance of success in this situation, and yet the principle of penalty-killing remains the same: to force passes and shots from the perimeter. To do that, you set up a triangle defense, with your forward at the apex and the two defensemen at the base. The forward will not be able to cover both point men, but he can shuttle between them and at least prevent them from rushing into the slot.

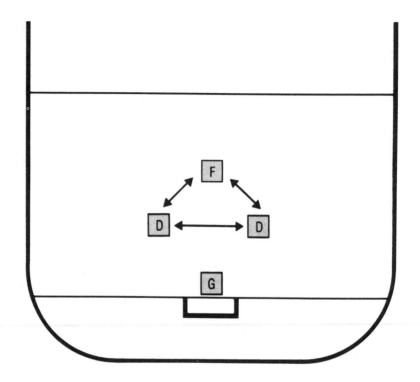

The two defensemen and the goalie are responsible for low coverage, with the strong-side defenseman confronting the puck carrier, the weak-side defenseman taking the man in the most dangerous shooting position and the goalie left to deal with the third forward. The goalie should also be prepared to freeze the puck (that is, hold onto it and get a whistle) at every opportunity, gaining a faceoff in which your team has a 50-50 chance of regaining possession and icing the puck.

DEFENSIVE-ZONE FACEOFFS

In a defensive-zone faceoff, your positioning is dictated by what your opponents do. If they line up straight across—that is, with a wing on either side of the center—then you will do the same in an alignment that looks like this:

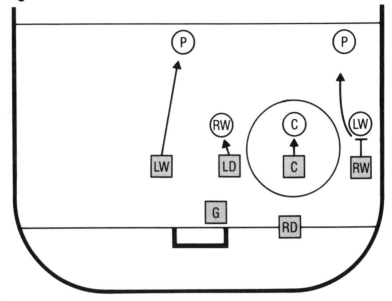

Here, your right wing covers their left wing and could also go up and cover the board-side point. Your left wing covers their right wing, your weak-side defenseman covers the slot and your strong-side defenseman is behind the center to trigger the breakout play should your team win the draw.

On the other hand, if your opponents drop a forward back into the high slot for a quick shot on goal, then you'll want to have both your wingers in front of the net in an alignment that would look like this:

Defensive zone coverage for the slot man.

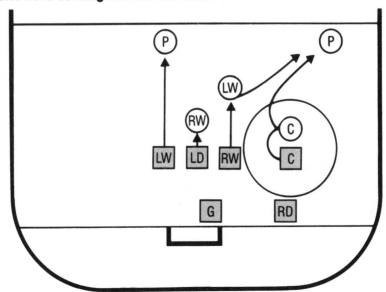

Here, your left wing (LW) can scoot out and cover their right wing (RW) should the draw go to him and continue out from there to cover the right point. Your RW can skate through to take the board-side point while, as always, one defenseman covers in front of the net and the other stays in the corner hoping to get the draw.

If you are a center and you lose the draw, then your responsibility is to check the other team's center and keep him from driving to the net.

CONCLUSION

Let's face it, left to your own inclinations, you would probably prefer to work on your offensive skills rather than on your defensive skills. Carrying the puck in on the goalie, shooting and scoring are the glamorous parts of the game, while defensive skills like body checking, shot blocking and working (hockey players call it "grinding") along the boards to regain possession of the puck is really the trench warfare of the game.

All the defensive skills in the book come into play when a team tries to kill a penalty. Since you can't defend man-to-man, you must shut off access to the key scoring zone, the slot.

Defensive players may not draw the plaudits of the crowd or the media attention that great offensive players get. But defensive play is as important to winning. In any game between two evenly matched sides, one team will probably have to play without the puck half the time. And in a case where a great defensive team meets a great offensive team—particularly in a championship—most experts would give the great defensive team the better chance of winning. This was clearly the case in the 1983 Stanley Cup finals, when the defending champion New York Islanders, an outstanding defensive team, beat the Edmonton Oilers, then the highest scoring team in the history of the NHL, 4 games to 0, thanks mainly to defense and goaltending. It wasn't until the freewheeling Oilers played tighter and tougher team defense that they were able to win the Stanley Cup. In fact, the Oilers began their march to their first championship with a 1-0 *defensive* masterpiece against the Islanders in Game 1 of the 1984 finals.

Offense may be more fun than defense, but it is not more fun than winning. If your goal is to become a *complete* hockey player and if your team has championship aspirations, then you and your teammates must spend time—roughly, half of every practice—working on your defensive skills. After all, some of the season's biggest goals might be the ones your opponents *don't* score.

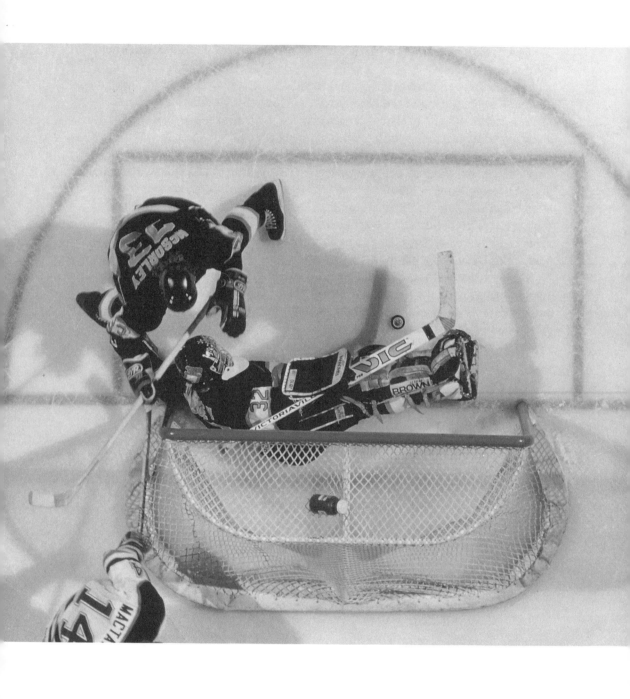

7

Goaltending

A Hall-of-Fame goaltender, the late Jacques Plante, once referred to goaltenders as "the craftsmen of hockey [who] besides doing their own work, have to correct everybody else's mistakes." He was right. The responsibilities of the goaltender are at least on a par with those of the baseball pitcher and the football quarterback. In addition, there is the ever present element of danger. Goalies risk being struck by a puck traveling at speeds of more than 100 miles per hour. Throw in the difficult techniques that a goaltender must master, and goaltending becomes one of the most demanding positions in team sports.

Despite the importance of goaltending, only recently have some professional and college teams begun using goalie coaches. Too often at the scholastic and youth levels, the goalie is left to learn this demanding trade on his own. He either manages to cope with its relentless pressures, or doesn't, and finds himself squeezed out of organized hockey. Fortunately, goaltending, more than any other position, lends itself to self-coaching. If you are a goaltender or aspire to be one, take heart: You will find that a disciplined, analytic mind will carry you farther, in the long run, than raw athletic ability. Don't be discouraged if you aren't playing the position as well as you'd like to be playing it. Instead, start to develop a clear picture in your mind of what the position requires of you and cultivate a self-correcting attitude so you can meet those requirements.

Of course, before you even *think* of skating out to protect the cage, you should be wearing proper equipment. That includes properly fitted skates, leg pads, knee pads, protective cup, pants, chest protector, long-sleeved vest, catching glove, backhand glove, mask, helmet, throat protector and stick. Let's look at what to consider when buying each.

157

Great goaltenders are masters of numerous difficult techniques. Here, the goaltender has performed a stacked-pads slide to prevent a score.

EQUIPMENT

Good equipment eliminates fear. No matter how brave and willing you are, enough hard shots to unprotected or poorly protected parts of your body will eventually make you afraid of the puck. That will affect the mechanics of your play and you will unconsciously begin flinching or lifting your body up and back. The moment you start to flinch, your effectiveness as a goalkeeper vanishes. To avoid becoming a cringing wimp in the net, you must make sure your equipment—head to toe—is the best you can afford.

Skates

On goalie skates, unlike regular hockey skates, the entire length of the blades touches the ice, to provide maximum stability. The blades are generally longer, and bars extend from the blade to the boot so that a puck cannot slip through.

Besides fitting well (see Chapter Two), a goalkeeper's boots should be well padded on the inside and outside of the foot, with the padding extending up and over your ankle bone. As we'll see, a goalie stops many pucks with the inside of his feet. Protection in this fragile area is a must.

Blade sharpening is an individual matter, but most goalies prefer slightly dull blades, which allow them to slide sideways without having the edge of the blade grabbing the ice. If your blades have just been sharpened, you can dull them with a carborundum stone (sold in most skate shops). Rub the stone lightly down the length of the blade. Or, if you discover during a game that your edges are too sharp, you can rub the blade lightly on the metal base of the goal.

Leg Pads

The maximum allowable width in leg pads is 10 inches when the pads are strapped to your legs, but the fact is that most pads flatten out to 11 inches or more as the season wears on and the pads wear down. Anything wider than that will make the pads difficult to control, particularly if the widest part is at the knees, which you must be able to snap together quickly to close up the "five hole." Height of the pads is an individual matter and depends on both the length and strength of your legs. As a rule, your pads should extend at least 3 inches over the top of your knees, so that the knees won't be exposed when you kneel.

Knee Pads

Even if your leg pad extends well over your knee there is still an area above the leg pad and below your thigh pad that is exposed when you kneel. Knee pads with hook-and-fleece fastenings should extend high enough above the knee to protect this area.

Protective Cup

Use a rubber-covered, boxer-style plastic cup for protection over a wide area and for less chance of slippage.

Pants

Goalie pants have extra padding sewn along the inside of the thigh, not only for protection but also to keep pucks from passing through. Your pant or girdle should also provide ample seat protection, since it is not unusual in the heat of play for a goalie to get knocked backwards onto the ice.

Chest and Arm Protection

Your chest protector, which has approximately the shape of a baseball catcher's chest protector, should not extend down beyond your waist or it will interfere with your movement. The long-sleeved vest must protect the *insides* of your arms and the area around your elbows, yet be light and flexible enough so that you can move easily. The top of the vest must protect your collarbone and the tips of your shoulders.

The Catching Glove

Catching gloves look like a baseball first baseman's mitt, with extra protection around the wrist. The best catching glove will 1) protect your hand, 2) allow you to catch the puck, and 3) permit you to *hold* everything you catch, that is, it will have a solid, flexible web and a deep pocket. The protective features to look for are ample padding around the wrist and across the back of the knuckles lest your catching hand be vulnerable to cuts and bruises from skates and sticks every time you use it to cover a loose puck.

After choosing a glove with a wide webbing and deep pocket you can improve these features by throwing a softball into your glove and by keeping the leather, including lacings, well-oiled. There are a number of commercial glove dressings on the market, but good old neatsfoot oil works as well as anything. Once your glove is broken in, to preserve the pocket, tie a softball, or four or five pucks, into the glove after each practice or game, and especially when you're going to be packing the glove in your equipment bag, where the weight of the rest of your gear might flatten it.

The Backhand Glove

The backhand glove, also called "the blocker," is the glove with which you hold the stick. The back of the glove (the part facing the shooter) is a flat rectangular pad (usually leather-covered fiberglass) with which you can block shots.

Select a glove that is lightweight and that gives you good protection on the thumb and at least some protection on the outside of the fingers with which you grasp the stick (these fingers are particularly vulnerable to quickly rising shots that get in under the big rectangular pad of your glove or that bounce up after hitting high on your stick).

Mask and Helmet

The trend in hockey today is away from the form-fitting, fiberglass mask (variations of the one introduced by Plante and, in recent years, made infamous by certain horror movies) toward cage-and-helmet combinations that offer more complete protection. The main objection to the form-fitting mask is that, while it will probably prevent the goalie from suffering wounds that require stitches or from losing teeth, such a mask rests so close to your skin that a hard shot will press the mask onto your face, an experience that is apt to be extremely painful and possibly injurious. Many youth and amateur leagues do not allow form-fitting masks, but some professional goalies wear them because they claim that, because the mask rests so close to their face, it does not interfere with their peripheral vision. If you do choose to wear this type of mask, make sure the padding (usually strips of rubber ¼-inch or less in thickness) will hold the mask away from your face at all points. If not, you can buy adhesive rubber strips and add padding where you need it. Also be sure the mask extends back far enough to protect your temples.

A cage mask will rest away from your face because it extends well beyond the helmet to which it is attached. Blows to the mask are cushioned by substantial padding around the chin. When trying on a mask, make sure that no part of the wire cage touches your face. An exceptionally hard shot could bend the wiring, allowing much of the force of the shot to reach your face. The best advice, in buying any mask, helmet or combination, is to be fitted by a qualified sporting goods dealer.

Throat Protector

It is impossible to react fast enough to prevent a deflected puck—particularly one tipped from right in front of you—from rising up and possibly hitting you in your one vulnerable spot, your throat. As shots get harder and deflections and screen shots become more popular, most goalies, including the majority of NHL goalies, are wearing throat protectors.

Your mask should come with a throat protector, a deflector pad that hangs from the bottom of the mask much as does the throat protector worn by catchers in baseball.

Stick

A goalie stick is roughly the shape of a regular hockey stick except that it has a blade that may be 3½ inches wide, and a widened portion of the lower shaft, which also has an allowable width of 3½ inches and may extend 26 inches up from the heel of the stick.

Tools of the trade.
A goaltender must learn to use—and move quickly in—about 40 pounds of specialized equipment.

Your goalie stick should be light enough for you to handle easily and without fatigue. Only experience will show you what lie is best for you but, in general, goaltenders who like to handle the puck a lot tend to prefer low lies (12 or 13), while others choose higher lies (perhaps 14 or 15) that are slightly better at helping you reach shots that are low to the stick side.

Passing and clearing are skills that are becoming increasingly important to modern goalies. For that reason, some of today's goalie sticks are manufactured with slightly curved blades (you are also less likely to lose the puck by having it roll off of the blade if the blade is curved). Another useful design innovation is a bend in the stick shaft just above the shoulders of the blade. This bend allows the goalkeeper to place the stick flush on the ice lengthwise. By contrast, a straight-shafted handle leaves a finger width of space when the stick is set on the ice, a small opening but a gap potentially large enough for a hard shot to force its way through.

When taping your stick, cover the entire blade, heel to toe, so that a shot hitting any part of the blade will have some of its force cushioned by the tape. Also, wind a small knob of tape around the top of the shaft so that the stick won't go sliding out of your hand when you attempt a poke check.

GOALKEEPING TECHNIQUES

The techniques of the goaltender are unique to that position. Many of your moves — such as the split skate save — are difficult to master. All must be done at top speed. In the pressure of a game, you won't have time to stop and think about mechanics. You must learn and practice each technique until you can perform it automatically. This usually means spending hours working with one shooter or, preferably, with a goalie coach. As you practice each technique, make sure the shooter or coach is not firing the puck at top speed. It is more important that you first learn the mechanics of each move, and that is easier to do against relatively slow shots. After you've mastered the mechanics, then you can work on your speed.

The Stance

Your basic stance is crucial because most of your moves are made from it. To get into a proper crouch, bend at the waist and keep your weight on the balls of your feet, your toes pointing slightly out, your knees flexed, your catching hand at about knee level with the glove held open, your backhand glove roughly even with the top of your leg pad and your stick blade flush on the ice. In effect, you are coiled and ready to spring in any direction.

The Stance

This is the basic goal-tender's stance from which all other moves are made. The goalie is square to the puck, comfortably bent at the waist, his knees are flexed, his stick blade flat on the ice, his catching glove open and he carries both gloves at about the height of the top of the leg pads.

Most goalies keep their legs close together though they don't always have the pads touching. A slight fanning out of the lower legs will create a small opening but will also allow you to split right or left a fraction of a second faster than you could if your legs were completely together.

Glove Saves

The catching glove is your best weapon because, with it, you can catch and control the puck. The most important principle in making a glove save is the old football receivers' and baseball fielders' maxim: Look It Into Your Hand — that is, keep your eye on the puck until it disappears in your glove. You may get away with "nonchalanting" a shot or two, but sooner or later the failure to keep your eye on the puck will cost you a goal.

After you have the puck, hold onto it and take a look around. If you can safely give the puck to a defenseman or drop it and pass it to another teammate, do so. But don't take chances. If there is an opposing player nearby, hold the puck and take a faceoff.

On slow shots high on your backhand side, you may have time to reach across your body and make the save with the catching glove using the backhand glove as insurance. A lot of young goalies will simply use the backhand glove to bat these shots away, but in so doing they give up rebounds. True, some shots come so quick or hard that all you have time for is a quick move with the backhand glove. In this case, your concerns are, first, to stop the shot with the big blocker pad on this glove and, second, at the moment of impact, to turn the rebound away from the goal.

Catching on the Backhand Side

Long or slow shots that come high on your backhand side give you time to reach across your body and catch, and, thereby, control them. Here, the goalie uses his catching glove for the save and his stick glove (or blocker) for insurance.

A

B

C

Save With Blocker

Hard or close-up shots to your backhand side often don't give you time to use your catching glove. Here, your first objective is to get your blocker in front of the shot for the save (A,B) and then to direct the rebound into the corner (C).

A

B

C

Leg-Pad Saves

On a shot directly into your leg pads, try bending your knees a little at the moment the puck hits the pad. This will cushion the force of the puck and thus cut down on the length of the rebound. If you do this properly the puck should drop close to you, where you can sweep it away with your stick or cover it. On a shot you must stretch to reach, you can control the rebound by directing the puck into the corner much as you do when you make a save with your backhand glove.

The leg pads are also used in sliding and "butterfly" saves, which we will discuss later.

Skate Saves

Your skates are your best defense against low shots to the far corners. In making a skate save, always turn your foot *outward* so that you take the shot on the *inside* of the blade or boot. The main thing to remember in making a skate save—whether it's the spectacular ballet-like split or just a little stand-up half-split—is to *keep your blade flush on the ice and turned to the outside so that the rebound won't come back out in front.* Split skate saves, wherein your legs split apart gymnastically, put a sudden strain on groin muscles, so make sure you do a few groin stretches before the start of each period of play.

The split-skate save.
Note that the goaltender's entire skate blade is on the ice and that the blade is turned slightly to deflect the puck to the side of the goal mouth.

Using the Stick

You use your stick mainly on shots that are headed for the gap between your feet or that are on your backhand side, too high for a split skate save and too low for a save with the backhand glove. As in all saves, stopping the puck is only half the job: You should then deflect the puck away from the goal. But your stick can do more than stop pucks. It can also help you prevent scoring chances. For example:

When the puck is behind the net and you are holding the post, you can use your stick to intercept opponents' centering passes. To do this, keep your skate blade up against the post and your body flush with the post to prevent pucks from squeezing in. You can then afford to hold out your stick blade, making it that much harder for opponents to pass the puck into the slot.

A

Holding the post.
The key to this technique is to jam your skate up against the goal post (A). To view the puck when it is behind the goal line, turn your head (B), not your body.

B

The Poke Check

This is a good move to use when the puck carrier has started to cut across in front of the goal and is within your stick's length. Note that the goaltender lets his stick slide up to the top of the shaft for maximum range.

The Cutoff

Here, the goaltender leaves his goal (A) to intercept a puck (B,C) as it comes around behind the net. Note that he stops the puck with his stickblade, not with his skates or pads, and that his eyes follow the puck all the way to the stick.

A

You can also use your stick to poke-check a player, stopping him before he gets off a shot. This is a good move to use on a player who is cutting across in front of your net. As the player makes his cut—and the puck is within a stick's length of you—*quickly* thrust out your stick, letting your hand slide all the way up the shaft for maximum extension. Aim the bottom of your stick blade *directly at the puck*. Some goalies add a few extra inches to their poke check by dropping to their knees and fanning out their leg pads as insurance against the opponent's avoiding the poke check and trying to slide the puck into one of the low corners.

As hockey has continued to open up, goalies have seen their tactical roles expand almost to a point where some are becoming "third defensemen," taking, making and intercepting passes. Stickhandling, passing and shooting (some goalies, like Philadelphia's Ron Hextall, have excellent shots with which they can fire the puck out of their zone) are difficult to do when you are wearing goalie gloves. The key, when handling the puck, is to slide your top hand up the shaft of your stick for greater control, and to use your catching glove to grip the stick high on the wide part of the shaft. A flexible, well-broken-in catching glove will help you get a firm grip on your stick.

There will also be times when you will have to leave your net to intercept a pass that is going behind the goal. That's a good move against a team that likes to dump the puck into your zone. Use the blade of your stick to stop the puck and then leave it a few inches away from the boards so that your defensemen can handle it smoothly and quickly.

B

C

Playing Angles

This is the most difficult part of goaltending. When, as a youngster, you first begin playing goal, making saves is often a simple matter of staying back in your net, waiting for your opponent to shoot, and then moving quickly enough to stop the shot. That system works well against young players who cannot shoot hard enough to overpower you. But as you move up the ladder, you will find yourself being beaten more often by opponents who can shoot faster than you can move. The only way to compensate for this is to learn how to come out of your net to reduce the shooting angle. Goaltending, at its highest levels, is less a matter of reflexes than of proper positioning. To put it another way: What you do before the shot is fired is more important than what you do afterwards.

The first thing you must do to play your angles properly is *keep square to the puck*. If an imaginary line extended from the center of the puck and another imaginary line went across your hips, those two lines should intersect at a right angle. Inexperienced goalies sometimes make the mistake of lining themselves up with the shooter's body rather than with the puck, giving the shooter more open net to aim for.

The question of how far out of the net to play is a more difficult one, and the answer depends in large part on game conditions. The main principle here is that the closer you move toward the puck, the less net is open and the greater the likelihood that the shooter will either hit you with the puck or miss the net in his effort to pick a corner. On the other hand, when you move out of your net you leave wide openings behind you. If the puck carrier beats you with a stickhandling move or passes to a teammate standing behind you, the result will almost certainly be a goal. As a rule, it is safe to come out when you are fairly certain of where the shot will be coming from. Let's say, for example, that a point man is in the act of shooting or an opposing winger must shoot from the boards because your defenseman won't let him cut in. In those cases, it is safe to come out and "challenge." But *if* the puck carrier is likely to pass or stickhandle or *if* he has a lot of skating room, you must be a little more conservative, coming out to about the top of the crease, far enough to reduce the angle somewhat but not so far that it's impossible to split or dive back to either post.

Knowing Where You Are

To play your angles properly you must know exactly where you are in relation to the net. That can be difficult when you are looking straight ahead and concentrating on the puck. Your best visual cue is the line delineating the crease. The

Playing the Angle

A goalie playing deep in his net (top) leaves a lot of open net for a shooter to aim at. The target area is reduced dramatically (bottom) as the goalie comes out a few feet in the direction of the puck.

increasingly popular semi-circular crease is more helpful than the rectangular crease because it extends further from the goal line, allowing you to move out further while still providing a frame of reference. But if the crease is faded, or you don't have time to glance down, or you know that you will be going out *beyond* the crease, you can check your position by reaching back (never look back) to tap the nearest post. Use your catching glove to tap the post on that side and the thin part of your stick shaft (not the blade) if you are standing nearer to the post on your backhand side. Feeling the post, even though you don't actually see it, will fix its position in your mind and reduce the chance that you will be off your angle as you move out.

Playing the Screen Shot

There will be times in a game when there will be so much traffic in front of you that you won't be able to see the puck and, therefore, won't know exactly where or how to play it. The most important thing to remember in this situation is to GET LOW. You can't see through players' bodies, but you might be able to get a glimpse of the puck through their legs. Don't make the mistake of straightening up and trying to look over players' shoulders—even if you locate the puck, you will be off balance and unable to move to make the save.

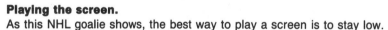

Playing the screen.
As this NHL goalie shows, the best way to play a screen is to stay low.

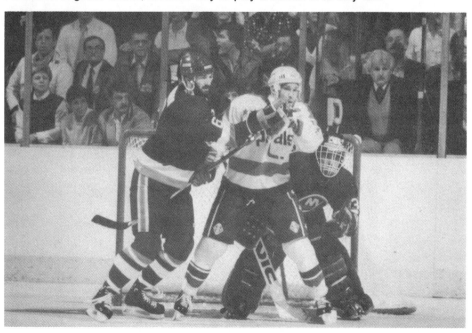

Some goalies play screen shots—and, indeed, many other shots—with a technique known variously as the "butterfly," the "V" or the "inverted split."

The Butterfly

In this move, you drop to your knees with your leg pads fanned out to cover the lower corners and with your hands ready to cover the top corners. This is sometimes a good all-purpose move, particularly on screen shots or shots that might be tipped from close range. But to do this successfully on a regular basis requires perfect timing (go down too soon and you will be defenseless against a pass or a fake—sometimes called a "deke"), excellent conditioning (because you will constantly be jumping up and down), and exceptional hand movement (to protect the top half of the net). Some goalies have used the butterfly style with great success, notably Hall-of-Famer Glenn Hall and ex-Chicago Black Hawks great Tony Esposito. But conventional goaltending wisdom and the ever-accelerating pace of the game argue in favor of a more conservative and mobile stand-up style, with the butterfly reserved for long screen shots, or for closing the "side door" on a player who is in the process of cutting around you.

The butterfly.
This move is useful in playing screened shots because, by fanning out his pads, the goalie covers most of the bottom of the net. The problem with the butterfly: It leaves the top corners exposed.

The Stacked-Pad Slide

This move—also called the pad-on-pad save—is an all-or-nothing technique in which you drop to the ice with one leg pad on top of the other and, hopefully, force the shooter to put the puck into your pads or body.

The stacked pad slide is best used when an opponent has the puck close to the open side of your net and you know you don't have time to skate across the goalmouth; or, when you see a chance to slide out into the puck carrier, catching him by surprise before he has a chance to shoot.

The keys to a successful stacked-pad slide are decisiveness and abandon. There can be no hesitancy or turning back. When you make up your mind to go down, drop to the ice quickly, aiming your knees at the puck. Get your lower pad and the full length of your body flush with the ice so that the shooter can't slide

The Stacked-Pad Slide

The stacked-pad slide is a useful move for getting across the goal mouth in time to stop a shooter who, otherwise, would be aiming at an empty net. Here, the goalie pushes from his right to his left (A,B) before dropping to the ice (C) and *quickly* extending his legs with one pad on top of the other (D) to form a wall in front of the shooter (E). This goalie also has his glove ready to try to catch a flip shot to the top of the goal.

A

B

C

D

E

the puck underneath you. Get your top pad on top of your bottom pad to present the shooter with the highest possible "wall." If you are going down on your stick side, keep your catching glove open and on top of your body and extend your stick along the ice at a right angle to the shooter, making it difficult for him to pass the puck in that direction. If you are going down on your catching-glove side, extend your catching hand along the ice as a barrier to attempted passes and get your stick and backhand glove *above* your body so that you are covering the widest possible area.

By now, I hope you can see that the technical moves required of a goaltender are not easy, and can be mastered only over a period of years. Added to these complexities is another side of goaltending, one that some players never master. That is coping with the anxiety and fear the position can produce.

COPING WITH ANXIETY AND FEAR

Goalies experience two kinds of concern: anxiety over their performance (the possibility of embarrassment is very real to all athletes but to none more so than to goalies), and the physical fear of getting hit by the puck. Most goaltenders will tell you that the pre-game anxiety they feel over how they will perform is worse than fear of the puck, but both feelings must be kept under control.

Pre-Game Anxiety

Pre-game anxiety serves a purpose. It alerts your mind and body to the stresses that are going to be placed on it. Ideally, anxiety keys you up to play at your best. It is better to go into a game with a few butterflies flapping in your stomach than with feelings of lethargy or overconfidence. Anxiety becomes a problem only if it gets so severe that it reduces your concentration or otherwise affects your play for the worse. If that happens frequently, you may want to consider playing another position.

Most anxiety can be controlled by mental discipline. Instead of letting your imagination take its own course, conjuring up images of all the negative things that *might* happen to you, use your pre-game time to think about your opponent, your game plan and what *you* want to do. How does the other team play? Does the opposition dump the puck or skate it in? Who are the big scorers you'll face? Does your coach want you to tie up the puck for faceoffs whenever possible, or does he want you to keep it in play? Focus on what *should* happen — *what you want to make happen* — not on what might happen. You will be less susceptible to nervousness if your mind is occupied with constructive thoughts.

Fear of the Puck

Fear of the puck is a slightly different matter. Goaltending requires a certain amount of courage, but it also requires the understanding that courage is not the total absence of fear but, rather, the ability to function well in spite of some fear. Every goalie knows how much it hurts to get hit with a puck in an unprotected part of his body, and every goaltender—like every skater—has to be aware that the possibility of serious injury in hockey does exist. However, as in the case of pre-game anxiety, it is only when your concern with being hurt begins to hinder your play that fear becomes a problem. What normally happens to a goaltender who becomes afraid of the puck is that he will start "lifting," straightening up from his crouch, ready for the high hard shot (the one with the greatest likelihood of hurting him) and content to play the low shot (the one with the greatest likelihood of scoring) as best he can. The problem is that a goalie who is lifting will be unable to play the low shots unless they are directly at him. If you find this happening to you, *concentrate on leaning forward*, keeping your stick blade on the ice (you can't lift and keep your blade on the ice) and moving out toward the shooter. You can also ask your coach to take a few half-speed shots at you in practice so that you can recover your confidence and polish your mechanics. However, if you can't rid yourself of fear of the puck and if, as a result, you frequently find yourself lifting, well, maybe goaltending isn't for you.

DRILLS

Most team drills that involve shots on goal will help you, too. But those drills are designed primarily for forwards and defensemen. As a goalie, you should have some drills of your own that will permit you to work on special techniques rather than simply stand there stopping pucks.

First, you should have a goaltending coach or an assistant coach who can work with you for a few minutes out of every team practice. The coach should be able to shoot accurately enough to place his shots in any given quarter of the net so that he can give you a succession of shots that will force you to repeat the same move—high on the stick side, low on the glove side, or wherever you feel you need work. These don't have to be hard shots. In fact, the shooter should not be blasting away at full power but should be shooting at half- to three-quarter speed so that you can concentrate on using the proper mechanics. Speed will come with experience and with the demands of the game. There are also several useful drills that you can do with a coach and one extra shooter. They are:

Cat and Mouse

A player or coach stands behind the goal with the puck while you hold the post and look back over your shoulder at the puck, just as you would in a real game. It is up to the puck carrier to try to score on you with a "wrap around"—that is by tucking the puck into the goal between you and the post. Your job is to move from post to post fast enough to stop him. The puck carrier should give you a lot of fakes to try to make you move the wrong way. This drill lets you work on your lateral movement, post-holding technique and overall mobility.

Pass Outs

This drill simulates a game condition in which a player behind the net tries to pass out to a teammate in the slot for a quick shot on goal. Your job is to block the attempted pass with your stick or, failing that, to move out quickly to play the shooter.

Rebounds and Deflections

Let one player or coach shoot on goal from 40 to 50 feet while another stands near the net ready to deflect the shot or to get the rebound and score. In the case of a deflection, you want to get as close as possible to the point where the player will tip the puck so that the deflected shot will go into your pads. If the shot is not tipped, you must concentrate not only on making the save but on preventing a dangerous rebound, either by holding onto the puck or deflecting it into the corner.

Cutoffs

This drill gives you a chance to practice your stick work. Have a shooter stand outside the blue line and shoot pucks into the corner so that the puck will carom around the boards and behind the net, just as it would if you were playing against a team that likes to dump the puck into the offensive zone. As the puck comes around behind the net you have to move from the goal and intercept it, leaving it a few inches from the boards just as you would in a game if you were leaving it for one of your defensemen. Make sure you learn to cut off shots coming both clockwise and counterclockwise. And—just to keep you honest—tell the shooter to take an occasional shot directly on goal.

The Cat-and-Mouse Drill

Here, a coach or player stickhandles back and forth behind the net, trying to score either by faking the goalie off the near post or by beating him to the far post. This drill helps the goalie work on lateral mobility, post-holding technique, and behind-the-net pursuit of the puck.

A

B

C

The Machine Gun

In this drill about a dozen of your teammates, each with a puck, stand in a semi-circle within a radius of about 50 feet. On a signal from you or a coach, the player at one end of the semi-circle shoots. As soon as you make that save, the player on the other end of the semi-circle shoots. Shooters keep alternating in rapid-fire succession until all the pucks have been shot. Then players retrieve the pucks and set up in another semi-circle, this time moving in a bit closer. This drill forces you to move quickly from right to left and to stay on your feet. For extra work on your skate and pad saves, try doing this drill without your stick.

A NOTE TO COACHES

Goalies are not cannon fodder. Drills involving high-rising shots from close range (particularly backhands), or that call for a goalie to lie on the ice while other players skate up to him and try to flip the puck into the top half of the net, are dangerous, demeaning and useless to the goalie. You can do these and any other potentially hazardous drills just as well with a shooting board or with a bench placed in front of the goal mouth. And you should allow time to let your goaltender and a shooter go to one corner of the rink and work on special skills. Your goaltender, and your team, will be better served.

A GAME APART

Whether you are crouched at the hub of that swirling pinwheel of action that is a hockey game or standing alone in front of your goal while that same pinwheel spins up ice, you, as a goalie, must realize that you are playing a position that sets you apart from your teammates. Even hockey's rules differentiate between "players" and "goaltenders." For example, NHL Rule 15, Section A, reads in part: ". . . the Manager or Coach of each team shall list the *players* and *goalkeepers* who shall be eligible. . ." (italics added). And, later in the same section, "Not more than eighteen players, *exclusive of goalkeepers*, shall be permitted" (Italics added).

But you are set apart by more than rules. Your equipment is different from that of your teammates, you are measured by a different set of statistics (wins, losses, goals-allowed average and save percentage rather than goals, assists and points), your practice requirements and coaching needs are different and the mechanics of your position call for you to master skills no other player needs. More important, you must shoulder a disproportionate share of responsibility for the outcome of the game and must do so in such a way that you are a calming, steadying influence on your teammates. Goal is a position for the mechanically sound and mentally strong.

Your mental strength is most severely tested—and your sense of "aloneness" most keenly felt—after a goal is scored.

You can't help feeling disappointed when you let in a goal. It is a natural human reaction. What you can and must avoid is allowing your feelings to guide your actions. A goalie who goes into a stick-smashing, referee-haranguing tantrum or a shoulder-drooping, head-hanging depression after being scored against is a goalie who projects an image of instability and who undermines his teammates' confidence in him. An excessively emotional reaction will also erode your own performance by taking your concentration from the game (where it belongs) and placing it on the goal that was scored (where it plainly does *not* belong). While you are thinking about the last goal, you may be giving up the next one, initiating a downward spiral that may cost your team the game.

You must accept the fact that goals *will* be scored against you. When they are, your attitude should be one of controlled aggressiveness. You have to realize that the only way to nullify the importance of the shot that beat you is to stop the next shot, and the shot after that, and to stop enough shots so that your team wins the game. You may not be able to completely control the way you *feel* but you can control the way you *act*. Here are a few dos and don'ts to guide your behavior in those crucial moments after a goal is scored:

1. *Don't* criticize your teammates even if the goal is someone else's fault. You can talk about it after the game or at practice. There is no point in undermining a teammate's confidence in the heat of a contest. Besides, it makes you look like a crybaby.

2. *Do* speak confidently if you speak at all. You can remind your teammates that there is plenty of time left for them to score, or that the score of the game is still close, or that your team traditionally plays well in the third period. The important thing is not what you say but that you think and speak positively.

3. *Don't* try to analyze the goal on the spot. Save that for when you talk to your coach or your teammates after the game or at practice. Keep your concentration where it belongs, on the play in front of you.

4. *Do* ignore distractions from the crowd. Goalies, particularly in college and pro games where crowds are large, are often the target of taunts and jeers from the stands. To acknowledge these is to allow yourself to be distracted and, in fact, to encourage further taunting and jeering.

As any pro will tell you, playing goal is never easy.

Still, few hockey experiences are more satisfying than a well-played game in goal.

At times it may seem unfair that a position requiring all the mechanical skills of goaltending is made even more difficult by its great mental demands. Yet few team sports offer satisfactions greater than that of knowing you have played well in this most difficult position. In those moments you will feel, as the game's rules suggest, that you are not just a "player." You are much more.

8

Conditioning

Skating ability and technical skills will make you a good hockey player, but they will never make you a *complete* hockey player. To be the best player you can be, you must enhance and support your mechanical skills by conditioning the two things those skills depend on—your body and your mind.

The days when hockey players could "play themselves into shape" are long gone. Today's high-speed game requires that you be in top physical shape whenever you play. Getting in shape for hockey means improving your endurance, strength and flexibility.

ENDURANCE

A highly skilled player who comes back to the bench "sucking wind" after a 45-second shift in the first period is unlikely to be of much use to his team in the latter stages of the third period, a time when teams and players with lesser skills but superior endurance can beat teams and players of greater skill but poor endurance. Tired players will not win those little one-on-one battles for the puck, which frequently decide the game.

To be at your best from start to finish means that your lungs, heart and blood vessels must be capable of delivering oxygen to your muscles *on demand*. Fatigue is caused when your body's demand for oxygen (the body's "fuel") exceeds supply. Endurance training means increasing the capacity and efficiency of your heart, lungs and blood vessels. Strong muscles are desirable, but your muscles won't do you any good if your body can't deliver the oxygen that drives them.

Hockey players need two kinds of endurance training—aerobic and anaerobic. Aerobic training conditions your heart and lungs for long periods of physical

185

Hockey is such a physically demanding game that only
the fit and flexible can hope to play it well.

Serious hockey players require both aerobic *and* anaerobic conditioning.

stress. Anaerobic (meaning, literally, "without air") conditions your body for short bursts of maximum energy alternating with brief periods of recovery. At the extremes, a marathoner would be said to have good aerobic capacity while a sprinter would be said to have good anaerobic capacity. Obviously, anaerobic training is critical to a hockey player, who often must skate all-out, but only for a few seconds, and whose 45-second shift is apt to be followed by 90 seconds or more of rest. Yet *aerobic* training is also extremely important because it provides the foundation for anaerobic conditioning. That is, aerobic conditioning, while it may not simulate what you encounter in a real game, is what builds the *capacity* of your heart and lung system. Good aerobic conditioning will: 1) increase your heart strength (so that your heart can pump more blood per stroke), 2) increase your lung capacity, 3) increase your circulation by raising the number of blood vessels carrying blood (and, therefore, oxygen) to your tissues and 4) increase the total blood volume in your body.

In general, aerobic training is a good off-season activity since it will help you

achieve a high level of heart-lung efficiency, thus making it easier for you to switch
to the anaerobic conditioning that makes up much of the pre-season (that is, the three or four weeks before on-ice practice) workouts of school, college and professional players. Note: Before embarking on this or any other fitness training, you should first have a thorough physical examination from your family physician.

Running is probably the most-traveled route to good aerobic conditioning, but bicycling, riding a stationary bike or skating on roller blades (a skate-like boot with a single "blade" of wheels attached) can also help you get in shape, and each has the added advantage of reducing the stress on knees and feet that running produces. Whatever activity you choose, the important thing to remember is that, for your workout to be beneficial, it must raise your heartbeat to at least 150 beats-per-minute and then maintain that or a higher rate for a minimum of 20 minutes. Anything less than that will not challenge your heart-lung system enough to strengthen it.

You can determine your heart rate by placing your fingers on your inside wrist at a point about an inch below the base of your thumb. To calculate your heart rate, count the number of beats you feel in a 6-second period, then multiply that by 10 to determine your heartbeats-per-minute. If your workout has been worthwhile your heart rate should be in the 150 to 170 range. Try to take your pulse immediately after you stop exercising. If you don't, you will probably get an inaccurate reading, since heart rates decrease quickly once exercise stops.

As the season draws closer, you will want to begin the transition toward anaerobic conditioning. One of the best methods of good anaerobic conditioning is a program of "interval training"—that is, brief periods of hard work alternating with brief periods of rest. This simulates the kind of off-and-on stress you'll encounter in a hockey game.

A fairly simple interval-training workout would call for:

1. A warm-up session of stretching and jogging.
2. Three 220-yard dashes (halfway around a standard track).
3. Three 100-yard dashes.
4. Three 40-yard dashes.

Your work-to-rest ratio should be about 1 to 2, that is, 2 units of rest for every 1 of work. For example, if you run your first 220-yard dash in 30 seconds, you should spend about one minute resting (walking slowly so that your legs don't stiffen) before running your next 220. A good rule of thumb is to rest until you stop panting.

Interval training four or five times per week for about three weeks before the start of on-ice training should put you in excellent shape for the demands of actually playing hockey.

STRENGTH

Weight Training

It got a lot of publicity a few years ago when Wayne Gretzky admitted that he was then one of the few NHL players who never lifted weights. But, after a few seasons in the NHL, even Gretzky had begun to strengthen himself through a weight training program. Indeed, the benefits of weight or "strength training" as it's sometimes called, are almost universally accepted at the scholastic, college and professional levels. Those benefits are: 1) decreased incidence of injury, 2) increased confidence and 3) increased physical capacity (strength, endurance, flexibility, power).

While weight training is an important part of the overall conditioning process for physically mature athletes, it is not recommended if you are under 15. Younger players who begin lifting weights run a great risk of overloading still-developing bones, muscles and joints.

According to Boston University Strength and Conditioning Coach Mike Boyle, who works with that school's NCAA Division I hockey team, the most important thing in beginning any weight training program is to learn proper technique from a qualified instructor. This will probably mean learning from a coach or physical education teacher at your school or from an instructor at a local health club. Other guidelines for the beginner are:

1. Always go through a complete passive stretching routine before any weight training session.

2. Don't attempt a maximum lift.

3. Never train alone. There is too much chance that your inexperience will lead to poor judgment, which could lead to an injury.

4. Do not look at weight training as competition. Emphasize your own steady improvement. Don't worry about what others are accomplishing.

Beyond these guidelines, your weight training program should be "complete," that is, it should exercise all the major muscles in your body—and it should be "simple," that is, the lifting techniques should not be terribly complex. For further information on how to tailor a weight program to meet your hockey-playing needs, see *Sports Illustrated STRENGTH TRAINING,* by John Garhammer (*Sports Illustrated Winner's Circle Books*, 1987). If you embark on a sound, well-supervised off-season strength program, you should see positive results the next time hockey season rolls around. But remember: For all of that strength and conditioning work to have the optimum effect on your game, it must be supported by a sound program of nutrition.

Playing hockey requires you to consume 3,000 to 6,000 calories per day. To maintain your playing weight while meeting the demands of the game, you will have to replace all of the calories your body burns. If you are a young and, therefore, a growing player, or even if you are a mature player who wants to gain weight, you must consume *more* calories than you burn. How, when and in what form you consume those calories will affect your playing performance. You cannot maintain your body's energy stores without a planned and balanced diet. Thus, if you have a working knowledge of basic nutrition you will have an advantage when competing against a player who lacks that knowledge.

The Four-Food Plan

It may seem simplistic—surely you have heard it before—but the most important nutritional factor is a balanced diet, that is, a diet made up of foods from the four basic groups: 1) dairy products, 2) meat (including fish and poultry), 3) fruits and vegetables and 4) breads, cereals and grains.

The mistake many athletes make is not that they don't eat foods from all four groups, but that they don't eat those foods in the proper ratios. Athletes have a

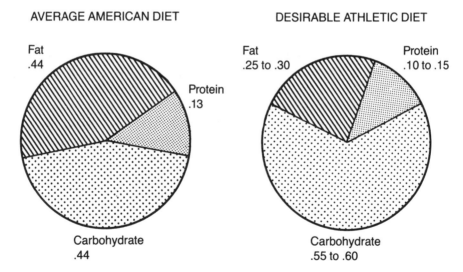

The average American diet vs. the athletic diet.
The typical American diet is too high in fat and too low in carbohydrates needed to power the body during strenuous activity.

tendency to neglect carbohydrates (breads, cereals, grains, fruits) in favor of a high-fat, high protein diet. The result is unwanted weight gain. While consuming some protein and some fat is necessary, it is carbohydrates that supply most of the energy used in hockey. The energy from carbohydrates is also more quickly available to you, since your body digests carbohydrates faster than it can digest fats and proteins. Today, most athletic trainers recommend that *more than half* of your daily caloric intake be in the form of carbohydrates.

Meals and Snacks

Three meals a day may be adequate for a non-athlete, but anyone playing a sport as demanding as hockey has to consume extra calories, in the form of second helpings, large portions or between-meal snacks. The key to intelligent, nutritious snacking is to avoid hard-to-digest foods like candy, potato chips or any fried food in favor of fresh fruits, granola bars or some of the liquid protein drinks currently on the market.

Besides avoiding "junk" (that is, high-sugar) foods, you should moderate your intake of fatty foods such as oils (including mayonnaise and salad dressing), whole milk products (substitute low-fat), eggs and red meat.

Liquids

There used to be a widely-held belief among coaches that athletes should restrict fluid intake during games and practices. Fortunately for the health and comfort of all athletes, that point of view has become generally discredited. It is important to replace body fluids lost through sweating, which is what your body is trying to tell you when it gets thirsty. Water and fruit juice are excellent ways of replacing the fluids your body has lost. Drink as much as you want when you want it.

The Pre-Game Meal

Contrary to what you might think, your pre-game meal is *not* crucial to building your energy stores. As some trainers tell their players, what you're playing on today is what you ate two days ago. But your pre-game meal *is* important for maintaining an adequate level of blood sugar and avoiding the sensation of weakness or hunger during the game.

You should eat your pre-game meal no later than 2½ to 4 hours before game time so that you will have time to digest the food.

Because carbohydrates are digested faster than fats, foods from the fruit, cereal and grain group are excellent pre-game choices. In recent years there has been a tendency for professional and college teams (those teams whose pre-game meals are planned by trainers or nutritionists) to substitute pasta for the traditional pre-game steak.

Try to drink two or three glasses of water or fruit juice with your meal to give your body an adequate fluid supply going into the game.

Now that endurance work, weight training and proper nutrition have your body in shape for hockey, there's only one thing left to work on—your mind.

THE MENTAL GAME

Proper mental preparation can help you in two ways: 1) by improving your concentration and 2) by enhancing your skill level.

Concentration—which is what coaches and athletes are really talking about when they use the phrase "mental toughness"—can be simply defined as keeping your mind on your job to the exclusion of all potential distractions, including your own anxiety, anger or other emotions.

To help them focus their minds on the game at hand and not have their concentration broken by pre-game anxiety or butterflies, sport psychologist Dr. Len Zaichowsky, consultant to Boston University's hockey team, advises that school's players to break the game down into segments. "Some of these segments" he explains, "involve things to concentrate on before the game such as mentally rehearsing different situations [more on mental rehearsal techniques in a moment] and making sure your sticks and skate edges are the way you want them." Then, as the game gets under way, Dr. Zaichowsky advises the players not to get emotionally caught up in the action as a fan would but to remind themselves of the key elements in each segment of their play—such as power-play responsibility, defensive-zone coverage, role in a breakout pattern—*before* starting a shift on the ice. "Don't overthink and get caught in what might be called paralysis by analysis," he warns. "Merely remind yourself of the two or three things you want to concentrate on, then let your trained body do the rest."

The point to remember here is that by forcing yourself to think about the specifics of the job at hand—the things you can and must control—you will not be distracted by negative thoughts about those things (the actions of teammates, fans, officials, etc.) that you can't control.

Mental Rehearsal

Mental rehearsal means using your imagination to recreate successful skill repetitions—to use your mind's eye to see yourself scoring a goal, making a save, hitting the open man on a breakout, and so on. Mental rehearsal is a means of programming the computer that is our subconscious mind. You envision the goal you are striving for, thereby telling your body what you expect it to achieve, and enhancing the chances that it will be achieved.

The advantage of mental rehearsal is that it can be done away from the rink (a major consideration to hockey players for whom practice ice is limited). It is a fact supported by research that mental rehearsal, when combined with physical practice, produces quicker skill acquisition than practice alone. And, beyond the advantage of improving your skill, mental rehearsal can reduce game-day anxiety and possible loss of poise by letting you experience and cope with the sights, sounds and emotions of stressful game situations *in advance*.

The best time for mental rehearsal is any "down time". While riding on the team (or school) bus, while resting after your pre-game meal, while sitting in the dressing room before a game.

The best mental rehearsal does not mean that you merely think about or visualize yourself performing a skill or coping with a situation, but that you actu-

Mental rehearsal.
Before a game, try to visualize yourself performing your skills perfectly. Such "mental rehearsals," sports psychologists tell us, can help you improve your actual play.

ally *reconstruct* the game venue—the sights, sounds, smell, climate and feelings you know you will experience when playing in a particular arena. These total imagined experiences must be seen through your eyes, felt through your limbs (particularly important if you're concentrating on a skill) and heard through your ears just as though you were on the ice.

For the best results from mental rehearsal, you should relax by taking a few deep breaths, sitting down, closing your eyes, and selecting the skills (for example, passing, receiving, shooting) game segments (breakout, power play, etc.) or situations (an uncalled foul against you in the late stages of a close game) that you want to reconstruct. See and feel yourself performing the skill or responding to the situation perfectly. Replay the skill or situation several times, each time concentrating on your own perfect performance. Remember, the more positive repetitions you have completed, the better you will perform a skill or handle a situation when you actually encounter it on the ice.

Poise

Poise, according to Ernest Hemingway's classic definition, is "grace under pressure."

According to psychologist Zaichowsky, there are three junctures in a game when you are most likely to lose your poise (and, thus, your concentration) and possibly cost your team a penalty, a goal, or the game: 1) after you've made a mistake such as giving up a goal or giving the puck away, 2) after a non-call by an official on what you thought should have been a penalty on an opponent and 3) after you've been fouled by an opponent. Zaichowsky's advice: "There simply is no reward in hockey for fighting (or otherwise losing your composure) so why do it? You want to be tough, aggressive, strong and intense but you want to be all of these with poise and self-control. When you make a mistake or get mad at the ref or at an opponent, do not lose control and take a cheap penalty . . . Instead, take a deep breath, say to yourself, 'self-control,' skate away from the situation and try to visualize that victory or championship and think of how good it feels."

Loss of poise translates to power plays for your opponents, and power-play goals are the deciding factor in many games at all levels.

SPORTSMANSHIP

Today, as a hockey player, you have a responsibility to your sport that probably exceeds that of any other athlete in any other sport. In the movies, on television

Clean play and a handshake for the opposition after a game—win, lose or draw—are two fundamentals of good sportsmanship.

and in some sports pages, people often see hockey players depicted as brawling goons quick to drop their sticks and put up their fists. The reality is that hockey is a swift, fluid and beautiful game when it is played—as it generally is—within the spirit of its rules. A recent study of NHL penalties shows that only 2 percent of the players account for 20 percent of all penalties. But hockey's image problem comes about as the result of the much-publicized fighting at the professional levels, the levels at which the game has the greatest number of viewers and, therefore, the greatest number of potential critics. However, fighting and all forms of violence start with—and will end with—the conduct of the players involved. Today's youth, scholastic and college players are tomorrow's professionals. It is at these lower levels of hockey that you, and all players, can continue to play hockey with respect for the rules and a reverence for the future of the game. The biggest fight in hockey is the game's struggle for widespread fan and media acceptance and respectability. It is a fight that you, and every player, can help win. Keep your head up, your stick down, your gloves on and, above all, keep skating.

9

The Volunteer Coach –
A Survival Manual

THE VOLUNTEER COACH –
A SURVIVAL MANUAL

Congratulations. If you are one of the tens of thousands of adults forgoing ski weekends, passing up fishing trips, postponing yardwork and otherwise giving up your leisure time to coach a youth team, then you should be acknowledged for what you are – the lifeblood of hockey. You make it possible for approximately 250,000 U.S. and 500,000 Canadian youngsters to play hockey in organized leagues. While the paid professional, collegiate or scholastic coach gets the most recognition, it is the volunteer coach of a youth team who teaches the basic skills, provides players with a foundation of tactical knowledge and often instills in the player a love for the game.

The "hockey boom" took place in the decade of the '70s; from 1969 to 1979, team registrations with AHAUS (the Amateur Hockey Association of the U.S. now USA Hockey) jumped from 4,255 to 10,933. Unfortunately, even to the present, the number of skilled, experienced coaches has not grown proportionately. Many adults who are more than willing to give their time to the game lack a background in organized hockey and may not be proficient in some of the skills they need to help their players learn. If you fit this category of volunteer coach, take heart. If you've read this far you already have a knowledge of the game's technical skills and tactical approaches. Often it is not the former brilliant player who makes the best coach but, rather, the person who had to struggle to learn the game and thus understands it better even though he may not be able to play it as well. The rest of this chapter will show you how, with your enthusiasm for the game, you can impart the knowledge you've already acquired to your players in such a way that you and your team will have organized practices, worthwhile games and an enjoyable season.

197

The lifeblood of hockey—
the volunteer coach.

AGE CLASSIFICATIONS

Most volunteer coaches work with very young players. Of the 15,450 teams registered with USA Hockey in 1991–92, 11,887 were made up of players under 17 years of age. While the term "pee wee" is often used to describe any young player, it should properly apply to only one of six classifications of players 19 and under. Those classifications are: Mites — age 9 and under; Squirts — ages 10 and 11 (10, 11 and 12 for girls); Pee Wee — 12 and 13 (13, 14, and 15 for girls); Bantam — 14 and 15 (there is no girls Bantam classification); Midget — 16 and 17 (16 through 19 for girls); Junior — 18 and 19 (there is no Junior classification for girls). Since Midgets and Juniors are often advanced players with scholastic, collegiate and, in some cases, professional aspirations, and since their coaches often have considerable experience and may, themselves, harbor professional aspirations, we will concern ourselves here with the coaching of teams in the Bantam, Pee Wee, Squirt and Mite classifications. These are the teams — particularly Squirts and Mites — to which new or less experienced coaches are often assigned.

ORGANIZATION OF TEAMS AND LEAGUES

Most community programs sponsor "house" teams and "traveling" teams. The house teams are made up of all the youngsters in the community who want to play. Let's take a hypothetical town program and call it Smithville Youth Hockey. Smithville may have 100 youngsters playing Pee Wee hockey. They could divide these youngsters — often via a coaches' draft so that the teams will be balanced — into five house teams of 20 players each, with the five teams playing against one another in the Smithville house league with no outside competition. The town, however, may also want to take its 20 or 40 or even 60 top players and form traveling teams, which will compete with traveling teams from other communities. There may, for example, be a Pee Wee A team made up of the top 13-year-old players and a Pee Wee B team made up of the best 12-year-old players.

Regardless of how your community program is structured, the important thing here is that the purpose of a house team is chiefly participatory, with great emphasis on a lot of playing time for all players and less emphasis on won-lost records and personal statistics. Ideally, that should also be the case with a traveling team, but, practically speaking, a traveling team is a representative team in the sense that it represents the town or in some cases a school. Thus, there is sometimes slightly more emphasis on a traveling team winning than there is for a house team. The coach should see to it that winning never becomes so important that he gives a handful of the top players most of the playing time while players of lesser ability languish on the bench.

To help eliminate the criticism directed at many youth sports programs (Little League baseball and Pop Warner football as well as youth hockey) for over emphasis on winning, and to move toward a national philosophy of youth hockey, USA Hockey has suggested the following guidelines for teams from Mites to Midgets:

THROUGH MIDGET AGE

A. There should be at least two practices for every one game that is played.

B. The following number of games would be recommended as season maximums: 1) 15 games for Mites; 2) 20 games for Squirts; 3) 30 games for Pee Wees; 4) 35 games for Bantams; and 5) 45 games for Midgets.

C. It is recommended that the Squirt teams and below play fewer than 3 games beyond a 10-mile radius from their program site.

D. It is recommended that the starting time for games be no later than:

Mites and Squirts—7 p.m.
Pee Wees—8 p.m.
Bantams—9 p.m.
Midgets—10 p.m.

Any practice time scheduled before 3 p.m. should be set so that the earliest times are given to the older age classifications.

E. Scoring records should be de-emphasized in the Mite, Squirt and Pee Wee age classifications.

F. Awards have become expensive and, in some cases, overdone. Any award program should be thought out so that players do not feel they will receive an award for just showing up.

G. It is recommended that each player of each team play a reasonable portion of each game.

While that code does not define "a reasonable portion" of a game, many youth coaches have a policy of changing lines and defense pairings on a sequential basis so that all players will end up with approximately equal ice time. It seems fair to say that it is these coaches who give the greatest number of players the opportunity to develop and to find pleasure in the game.

Of course, even a coach who believes in equal playing time for all players will not be able to provide much more than 15 minutes of ice time per player per game (exclusive of goaltenders, who often play half a game or all of every other game). And if a coach plays four lines in a strict 1-2-3-4 rotation through three 15-minute periods, that averages out to only 11 minutes, 15 seconds of ice time per player. Thus, team practices are far more important than games for providing players with the opportunity to develop individual and team skills. One of the most important jobs you have as coach of a youth team is the planning and running of practices. Before we get to the specifics of how to organize a practice, however, there are a few general principles you should adhere to:

1. *You should have* some *skating ability.* Even if you only played pond hockey as a youngster you should at least be able to go out on the ice to direct drills, communicate with your players and control practice. Most youth team programs require that players go through a learn-to-skate program before they are assigned to a hockey team. Therefore, most of your players should be grounded in the fundamentals of skating before they come to you. Your job will be to see that skating drills are a part of every practice. If you feel that your team needs further skating instruction and that such coaching is beyond your range, you might be able to prevail upon one of the program's skating instructors to give an occasional clinic or perhaps ask one of the better skating senior coaches in your program to offer skating instruction and conduct drills for 15 or 20 minutes at one of your practices.

2. *Don't fake it.* Be yourself. Don't pretend to be a hockey genius, particularly if you are a new coach in the program or if you never played much organized hockey. Your players look to you primarily as a *leader*, not as a hockey wizard. Level with the kids. If you're new to coaching, just tell them that you and they will be learning the game together and that you want to have fun doing it. You can improve your tactical knowledge very quickly by studying books and by attending coaches clinics, which are usually brief (a few hours to one-day) seminars conducted by top scholastic and collegiate coaches in your area.

3. *Be organized.* Ice time is expensive and is tightly scheduled. You probably won't have more than two one-hour practices per week. You can't afford to waste them. You should have a written plan for each practice (we'll show you a sample plan soon). Some coaches post their practice plan in the dressing room so that the players will know exactly what will be expected of them that day.

4. *Have a puck for every player.* If you were teaching history instead of coaching hockey and if your class had to share one book among every four or five students, you would quickly realize that there wouldn't be much learning going on. It is only when a young player is struggling to control the puck, to coordinate his movements with it, that stickhandling, shooting and passing skills improve. A puck is a motivator, teacher and disciplinarian wrapped up in one package.

Practices should stress fundamentals, such as solid skating skills.

Pucks are also inexpensive. They cost between 50 cents and one dollar apiece and should be provided by your community program.

With these points in mind, let's go to practice.

RUNNING A PRACTICE

What You Need

Besides your personal equipment (skates, stick, shin pads, protective cup and perhaps some gloves) you should bring the pucks (a plastic bucket is useful for carrying these), a whistle (not as an authority symbol but because the acoustics in most rinks are terrible), a padlock and key to secure the dressing room, and some plastic or rubber cones for drills, unless these are supplied by the rink. Of course, it is not absolutely necessary that you wear pads, but the fact is that there are a lot of flying pucks and fast-moving bodies at a hockey practice and, in the matter or protection, as the saying goes, it's better to have it and not need it than to need it and not have it.

Allocating Your Ice Time

Most youth team practices last precisely one hour because most rinks rent ice in 60-minute blocks. Because of this tight scheduling, a hockey coach does not have the luxury of keeping his team at practice an extra 15 or 20 minutes as would a football, baseball or basketball coach who might feel his team needs extra work. Furthermore, with ice fees in the $100-an-hour (or more) range, your team probably won't be able to afford more than two or, at most, three practices per week. Given these constraints it is incumbent upon you, the coach, to be thoroughly organized to get the most out of each minute of practice. Here are some suggestions as to what to do and how long to do it.

Stretching. At least the first 5 minutes of each practice should be spent getting the players to stretch out the muscles they are going to use.

Groin stretch—Even before the players begin skating they can go over to the boards, place one leg up on the dasher board (provided the players are tall enough to do this without straining the leg or groin muscle) and, while facing the stands, lean forward slightly, gradually increasing the pressure on the groin and slowly stretching it out. Warn your players not to do this to a point where the groin hurts, but merely to the point where they can feel the muscle stretching. Then have them switch legs so that the groin is stretched on both sides.

Now have your players skate slowly (hard skating comes later) around the rink while doing the rest of their stretches.

Wrist—Hold the stick in one hand at the midpoint of the shaft and give it a series (a dozen or so) of twists of roughly 180 degrees or to maximum comfortable extension. Twist the stick clockwise and counterclockwise. Switch hands and repeat.

Neck—Have players roll their heads slowly in big circles, clockwise and counterclockwise.

Groin (a useful stretch for players too small to get their legs up on the boards comfortably)—Have players glide with both blades on the ice while slowly spreading their legs apart and drawing them back together. They should gradually extend their leg spread (but never to the point of pain) as the groin muscles stretch out.

Leg and hip—Have your players hold their sticks in front of them horizontally. Now have them kick the end of the stick with the toe of their skate, alternating feet. Have them start with their sticks held *low* enough so that the kicks will only stretch (not strain) the legs. As the muscles stretch, they can lift their sticks higher, increasing the height of each kick. The "kick" here is more a deliberate raising of the leg than a violent thrust.

Another stretch that benefits the hip, leg and groin is to have players glide forward on one foot while stretching the other foot out behind them. Hold each leg extension for 3 to 4 seconds.

Pregame Stretches

The groin stretch.
The player on the left stretches his groin muscles by spreading his legs apart, then slowly drawing them together. This is an especially good exercise for smaller players who may not be able to lift their legs to the height of the dasher board to stretch without risking a muscle pull. Taller players, such as the one on the right, can stretch groin and leg muscles by lifting each leg up to the dasher board.

The wrist roll.
Twist clockwise and counterclockwise. Alternate hands.

Pregame Stretches (Cont.)

The neck roll.
Roll your head *slowly*, beginning with small circles and moving gradually to larger ones. Rotate clockwise and counter-clockwise.

The leg and hip stretch.
Start with a few easy kicks, holding your stick below waist level. As your muscles loosen, raise your stick and heighten your kicks.

The shoulder, back and torso stretch.
By pushing his arms against his stick, this player stretches most of the large muscle groups in his upper body.

Torso and shoulders—Have your players put their sticks over their shoulders and drape their arms over their sticks. By pushing their arms against the sticks they can slowly twist their upper bodies back and forth.

Back stretch—Players will have to stop skating to do this stretch, and it's not a stretch you want them to try if the ice surface is wet. But if the ice is dry you can ask players to lie on their backs while keeping their legs together and *slowly* lifting both legs up over their heads and down toward the ice.

Now that your players are warmed up and stretched out, you're ready to make the best and safest use of the rest of your ice time.

Skating Drills. The second phase of practice—say, 10 to 15 minutes of our hypothetical 60-minute practice—should emphasize skating, but these drills should not be so long or demanding as to fatigue the players. Conditioning is something you work on at the *end* of practice. Fatigue will reduce your players' attention spans and increase their risk of injury.

Drills should vary from practice to practice to avoid boredom. Here's one drill that is particularly useful because it has all of your players crossing over in both directions while skating both forward and backward.

Line your players up in one corner of the rink and, at intervals of about three seconds, have them skate the five circles in the sequence shown in the illustration below:

The five-circle skate.
Players skate the circles both forward and backwards, and in the process develop all their skating skills.

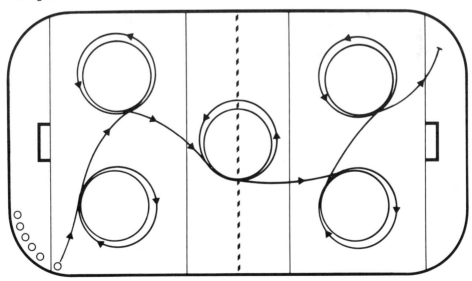

To make the drill more interesting and to help improve your players' stickhandling, you can let each player dribble a puck the second time he goes through the drill.

Skating in a giant, rink-length figure 8 and skating through a "slalom course" of rubber cones are also useful drills, provided you watch your players closely to make sure they skate (and don't coast) through the turns.

Your players can also work on foreward and backward skating and pivots by skating in a large circle around the rink, pivoting clockwise at one blue line and skating backwards, pivoting clockwise at the second blue line and skating forward, and then, as they come around to the blue line again, doing the same thing but pivoting counterclockwise.

Skill Sessions. With stretching and skating having consumed 15 to 20 minutes of practice, your players will be physically and mentally ready to move on to something they no doubt will regard as more fun, skill work.

In this middle portion of your practice you should spend about 15 to 20 minutes (more in the case of Mites and Squirts) working on basic hockey skills—stickhandling, passing, receiving, shooting. If your drills will involve shots on goal, then you should take a few minutes to let your goalies get warmed up. Ask your players to take long shots—say, from out at the blue line—then gradually move in closer. Goalies need a few minutes to get their timing right. If the first shots he sees each day are hard ones from 15 or 20 feet, it isn't going to help the goalie's confidence or his timing. Here's one drill that will help your goalie get warmed up while giving your other players a chance to work on passing and receiving:

Here, the first player in line, 1, passes up to 2. 2 passes to 4. 4 passes to 3. Meanwhile, 1 has skated around 3 and is heading toward the blue line. 3 passes to 1, who then shoots on goal and skates to the end of a new line of players that will form in the right-hand corner of the rink.

If a particular skill drill involves only stickhandling and passing, or if your players are shooting at the plywood target board, then this is a good time for the goaltenders to work with the goalie coach or, if you don't have a goalie coach, to work with one shooter practicing whatever shots the goalie and you feel he should work on.

In planning your skill drills or any other portion of your practice, keep in mind that players get bored quickly, at which point learning decreases and performance often falls off. Therefore you would do well to run through a succession of drills, with each drill lasting no longer than 4 or 5 minutes. You should also plan to progress from simple drills involving individual skills (such as stickhandling through a slalom course of cones) to the more complex, team-oriented drills, such as 2-on-1 and 3-on-2 rushes.

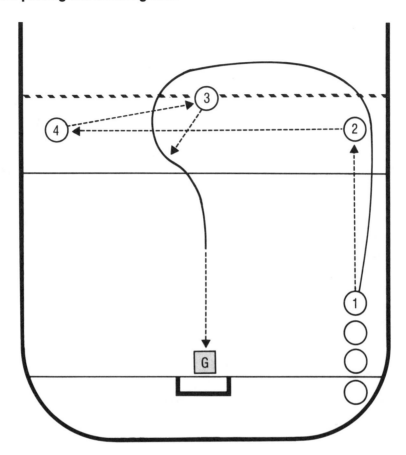

Game-Situation Drills. Approximately 15 to 20 minutes (more for older players – Pee Wees and up – less for younger) should be spent practicing game situations, such as power plays, penalty-killing, breakout plays, and coverage in the offensive and defensive zones.

Every practice should include work on your team's most important play – the breakout. If your players can't get the puck out of their defensive zone, they won't have the chance to win many games. After you've worked on the breakout (see Chapter Five), you might decide to let your players scrimmage for a few minutes, in which case you should have the players wear scrimmage vests (inexpensive sleeveless jerseys easily put on over the regular practice jersey) so that you and your players can easily differentiate players on one team from players on the other.

You can incorporate power-play and penalty-killing work into your scrimmage by setting aside a minute or two in which your team's power-play unit plays against the penalty-killing unit.

Conditioning. The final 5 to 10 minutes of your practice should be spent on conditioning drills. For example, there is the now-famous "Herbies" drill, so-named by members of the 1980 U.S. Olympic Gold Medal winners whose coach, Herb Brooks, used the drill frequently. Players line up on the boards at one end of the rink and, at the sound of the whistle, sprint forward. At the second whistle the players stop and reverse direction, sprinting back in the direction they just came from. At each whistle (usually blown at intervals of 2 to 5 seconds) players stop and reverse direction.

Another useful conditioning drill is to divide the team into four or five lines of four to five players each at one end of the rink. On the whistle, the first player in each line skates to the far blue line, stops, skates back to the red line, stops, skates again to the far blue line, stops, skates back to the near blue line, stops, then skates all the way to the far end of the rink, as shown below. Or, in a simpler version: far blue line, red line and then to opposite end of rink.

These drills simulate the constant stop-go-and-reverse-direction type of skating that players experience in a real game.

A conditioning drill.

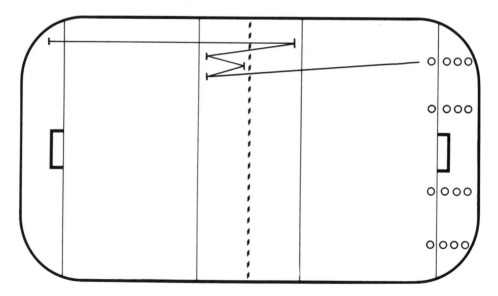

While all practice schedules must be tailored to the needs of the team and while schedules should vary from practice to practice to prevent boredom from setting in, a fairly typical practice for, say, a Pee Wee team, might look like this:

Stretch: **5 minutes**

Skate: **10 minutes**
1. Clockwise, skate backwards between blue lines.
2. Counterclockwise, skate backwards between blue lines.
3. Circle skate forward and backward, with and without pucks.

Skill Work: **20 minutes**
4 minutes goalie warmup
4 minutes 1-on-1 (sometimes have defensemen play without sticks)
4 minutes 2-on-0 (drop pass on first rush, shoot off pass on next rush)
4 minutes 2-on-1
4 minutes 3-on-2

Game Conditions: **20 minutes**
10 minutes breakout plays (at first with no forecheckers, then with one, two or three forecheckers to make the drill more interesting and realistic)
10 minutes scrimmage

Conditioning: **5 minutes**
Including final minute or two of light, easy skating as a warmdown.

THE PSYCHOLOGY OF COACHING

While those who have trained to become scholastic coaches or teacher-coaches often take Psychology of Coaching courses as part of their undergraduate work, most youth hockey coaches are professionals in other (non-educational) fields and have had little exposure to the subject. While a book of this size and scope could not presume to present a complete course on the psychology of coaching, there are a few principles you should be aware of, which are made available here through the assistance of Sports Psychologist Dr. Leonard Zaichowsky of Boston University.

The most important point to keep in mind when coaching youngsters is that what you are ultimately dealing with and influencing is the self-esteem of your players. The opinions most of us hold of ourselves – our self-esteem – are formed in large part by the way we see others responding to us. The words and actions you use in coaching your players will tell them what you think of them and will to some degree (varying with the individual player) determine what they think of themselves. Of course, all of your actions as coach will also determine how the players regard you, which, in turn, influences the extent to which they will respond to you as a leader and a teacher. Some advice for communicating with your players:

1. Communicate *positively* – Telling a player, "You'll get that slap shot off a little quicker if you shorten your backswing," is better than shouting, "What's the matter with you? It doesn't take all day to get off a slapshot."

2. Send messages high in specific information, low in generalities – Telling your team, "Okay, we're down by a goal and it's getting late so we'll go to a two-forechecker system," is better than telling them, "We've got to generate more offense." A study done of John Wooden, legendary former basketball coach at UCLA, showed that his verbal communication at a typical practice broke down to 75 percent specific instruction to athletes, 12 percent requests to hustle, 7 percent praise and 6 percent scolding.

3. Listen – Don't assume that because your players are young they have nothing to say. If you don't listen to them they may not listen to you.

4. Be consistent – Don't ask your players to contain their emotions after you've just thrown a tantrum at the officials.

Consistency is also the key to dealing with misbehavior. One of the most unpleasant facets of coaching involves discipline and punishment. Here are some guidelines that, while not making the disciplining of a player any more pleasant, will at least help you to make your own policies and procedures fair and consistent:

1. Limit potential misbehavior by clearly establishing behavior guidelines. Involve players in establishing these guidelines, and do so early in the season.

2. Never use punishment to retaliate against a player and, therefore, to make you feel better.

3. Allow a player time to explain his actions.

4. Don't lecture or embarrass a player in front of the team.

5. Select an appropriate punishment (for example, an apology to the offended party, repair or replacement of anything damaged or stolen).

6. Don't make athletes feel that they are in the "dog house." When the incident is resolved, forget it.

7. Avoid punishing for errors in play.

8. Never use physical activity (running laps, doing pushups, etc.) as punishment.

9. Punish sparingly.

Keep in mind that the most important needs of your players are to have fun and to feel worthy. You will help them toward those ends by dealing with them positively and fairly and by teaching them that success means achieving personal goals—progressing as a player and as a person—and is not measured by the won-lost record.

10

Building a Rink of Your Own

Ice time. It is your most pressing need and your biggest expense. Without it you will not—cannot—develop the skating skill you need to progress as a hockey player. But with many rinks charging hourly rental fees of more than $100, you and your teammates will probably be limited in the amount of practice time available to you, particularly if you are at the youth level, where most ice fees come out of parent's pockets, not school department athletic budgets.

Skating on natural ice—frozen lakes and ponds—is one solution and, for a portion of each year, a good one. But you can't depend on the quality or availability of natural ice. That perfect black ice that forms in the late fall is too soon covered with snow, or marred by cracks, leaves, twigs and debris. While you cannot count on having all the natural ice you want or need, however, you might be able to solve the problem by making a low-cost rink of your own. A lot of people do it.

Probably the most famous backyard rink in the world was built by Wayne Gretzky's father, Walter, out behind the family home in Brantford, Ontario. Walter used a sprinkler to flood a low flat area of the yard. Snow formed the walls and the cold Canadian winter took care of the ice-making.

Other, more elaborate, backyard rink designs call for wooden boards, a plastic liner, goal cages and even lights. These rinks are, almost by definition, makeshift affairs, and chances are that no two are exactly alike. But here is one design for an easily constructed, low-cost backyard rink, which, while it may not turn you into another Wayne Gretzky, should provide you with several years of those two most precious commodities—ice time and fun.

The author in his domain: an easy-to-build backyard rink.

ONE FAMILY'S RINK

For the past several years my family has built a 56 × 32 foot rink in the backyard of our home in eastern Massachusetts. We generally have ice from shortly before Christmas until the last week of February, although some years we have begun skating as early as December 15 and kept our ice until March 1. Here's how you can build a similar rink.

To begin, you need a relatively flat area of yard. Our rink has about an 11-inch variance from the shallowest to the deepest part. We suspect that much more of a difference would mean that the expanding ice would put excessive pressure on the boards, perhaps pushing them back or breaking them and ripping the plastic liner, and that the deepest part of the rink might take too long to freeze. As it is, our ice isn't ready to skate on until we have had three consecutive nights of temperatures at most in the low teens.

Once you select your area, examine it for rocks, exposed roots, twigs or anything that might puncture the plastic liner. We always let our grass grow extra-long in the fall to cover any pebbles or other small pieces of debris.

You will have to spend some money on wood and plastic, but the plywood and 2 × 4s you need to make your boards will only be a onetime expense, since you can re-use the boards each year. The plastic liner, however, will get torn and will have to be replaced annually.

To build a 56 × 32 ft. rink with boards, go to a lumber yard or building supply store and buy 14 4 × 8 (standard size) sheets of rough-grade half-inch-wide plywood. Also buy a roll of 6-mil. (the measure of thickness) clear plastic 40 feet wide and at least 60 feet long. (We buy a 40 × 100 ft. roll and always find uses for the extra material around the house and garden.)

Have the dealer cut nine of the plywood boards in half lengthwise to give you 18 2×8 sheets. The five large sheets will be for the boards behind the goal, while 17 of the 2-ft.-high ones (six on each side, five at the end) will form the walls of the rest of the rink. There will be one extra 2 × 8 ft. board. We use ours as a walkway from porch to rink. Of course, you could have 4-ft.-high boards all the way around or at both ends of the rink—if you're planning to have two goals—but this will add to your cost and make snow removal more difficult.

You will also need ten 10-ft. lengths and 34 3½-ft. lengths of 2 × 4s. With this lumber, you're ready to make your rink boards.

Nail one of the 10-ft. 2 × 4s to each end of the large sheets of plywood so that two feet of the 2 × 4 extends below the board (the 2 × 4 serves as a post to anchor the board in the ground). The remaining 4 feet of 2 × 4 rises above the board, and you will nail your screen backstop against it. The finished board—before you put it in the ground—should look like this:

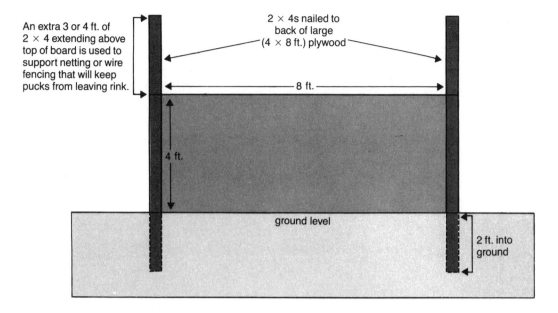

An extra 3 or 4 ft. of 2 × 4 extending above top of board is used to support netting or wire fencing that will keep pucks from leaving rink.

2 × 4s nailed to back of large (4 × 8 ft.) plywood

8 ft.

4 ft.

ground level

2 ft. into ground

Rear view: large board.

Now take the small 2 × 8 sheets of plywood and nail a 3½ ft. length of 2 × 4 to each end so that one end of the 2 × 4 is flush with the top edge of the board while the other end of the 2 × 4 extends 18 inches below the bottom of the board to serve as the board's leg. A finished board should look like this:

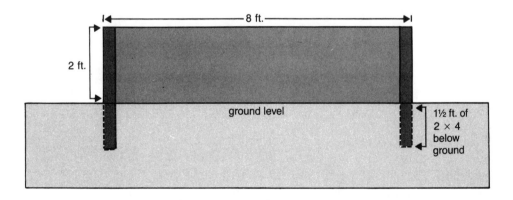

8 ft.

2 ft.

ground level

1½ ft. of 2 × 4 below ground

Rear view: small board.

Now comes the hard part: putting up the boards. Starting in the fall, well before the ground freezes, you will have to dig post holes so that you can set your boards in place. Each hole for the large (4-ft.-high) boards has to be at least 2 feet deep to allow the bottom of the board to be flush with the ground when the board is lowered in place. The holes for the 2-ft.-high boards need only be 1½ feet deep. Obviously, one post hole can accommodate two board legs. The ends of the boards should be touching each other, to create the smoothest possible seam. As you fill in the holes to secure each board, make sure you tamp down the earth *hard* to anchor the board securely. Also, remove any large or sharp stones you may have unearthed, so that these won't puncture your plastic. Here is a side-view of three lengths of board set in place:

Side view of three lengths of board set in place.

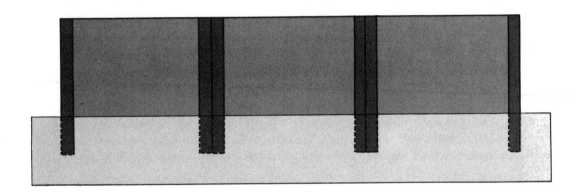

Digging post holes is a demanding, tiring job and not something you want to try to get done in one day, at least not unless you have a lot of help. We put up our boards over a period of five or six days, minimizing the drudgery and fatigue.

When your boards are all in place you will have made a kind of plywood "corral." But because your seams (that is, the juncture of two boards) will not be perfectly flush, you will have to cover them with other material. That should prevent your plastic from being ripped on the rough edge of an exposed board or forced out and ruptured through a small gap in the boards by the pressure of the water. We use a variety of materials to smooth over these seams: Old towels, pieces of sailcloth and sections of old carpeting work particularly well. Cut a piece of material about 6 to 12 inches wide (wide enough to cover the seam) and high enough to extend above the anticipated water level. Nail these in place over each seam.

Material nailed over board seams.

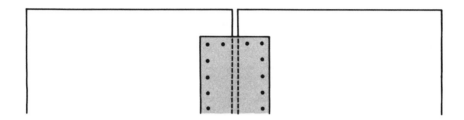

Since your yard is probably uneven, there may be some large gaps where the bottoms of some boards are not perfectly flush with the ground. You can fill these in using any soft material, such as rags, or whatever you have left over after you've sealed the seams in the boards. Place this material *inside* the rink where it will cushion the plastic liner and keep it from being forced out under the boards by the water.

When your basic "corral" is up, you may want to buy a roll of lightweight garden wire (something heavier than chicken wire but lighter than chain link) to raise the height of your backstop. Obviously, the mesh in the fencing should be small enough so that a puck will not go through it. Put the wire backstop in place by nailing it to the 2 × 4s that stick up above the five large plywood boards. A fence 3 or 4 feet high will appreciably reduce the number of pucks you lose in the course of a winter—though nothing more quickly teaches a young hockey player the value of keeping his shot down than the long tramp through the deep snow to retrieve shots that went over the net and out of the rink.

Now comes the easy part. Wait for cold weather, not those first teasing nips of winter that leave frost on your windows, but a good three-day or more deep freeze with nighttime lows in the teens, daytime highs below freezing and slim prospects of snow for at least the first 48 hours—the time when you'll be making ice. The problem with snow during ice-making is that your ice may be just thick enough to support the snow, but not thick enough to support a person with a shovel. Thus, you will have ice too thin to skate on, and will have no means of cleaning it off.

When you're fairly certain that a frigid stretch is on the way, you're ready to put the plastic liner inside the boards. We lay the plastic the same day we flood because to do so earlier is to run the considerable risk of having the plastic torn before it is filled with water. Unroll the plastic, spread it out, trying not to step on it, and secure it by stapling it to the sides of the rink. Make sure it extends far enough up the boards to remain above the expected water level. Now you're ready to flood your rink.

We place a garden hose near the boards at the deep end of the rink (in local vernacular the deep end is called the "shooting" end) and let the water run until the entire rink is filled to a depth of at least 2 inches at the shallowest point. That usually takes about 10 to 12 hours.

Now comes an even easier part: Put the hose away and wait for the water to freeze. But wait *patiently*. It may take three days before the ice is thick enough to skate on. A hole in the middle of your ice made by an overeager skater can be a tough repair job, and a nearly impossible one if a skate blade goes through the ice and rips the plastic liner.

Once the ice is ready, you'll have a lot more fun on your rink if you can buy an old goal cage (we got one from a local rink) or, failing that, if you can make one yourself out of 2 × 4s or other scrap lumber.

RESURFACING

After an hour or so of skating, your ice will need resurfacing. First, scrape off the accumulated snow with a shovel (the First Commandment of rink ownership as regards all skaters is: If You Skate, You Must Help Shovel). Then set the hose nozzle for a medium spray and, starting at one end of the rink, gradually spray a thin layer of water over the entire rink surface. That layer will freeze quickly, giving you good-as-new ice. Night is the best time to resurface—temperatures are colder. Avoid trying to resurface in the daytime if the temperature is just below freezing and the sun is shining on the ice.

As you use your rink, tears in its plastic, caused by sticks, skates and pucks, are inevitable but all of these cuts will probably be above the water line, and therefore should not affect the quality of your ice or the water-retention qualities of the plastic itself.

If you have electrical outlets available outdoors, you might want to rig up some lights so that you can use your rink at night (you will also appreciate the extra light when you're resurfacing it). We light our rink with four 150-watt floodlights mounted on the side of a garage. It's not the Boston Garden, but our backyard "Omni" has seen some wonderful neighborhood scrimmages.

The pleasures and rewards of a backyard rink—for parents and children—are numerous.

Eventually—in late February for us—the days grow longer and warmer and the ice begins to melt. When that happens, we just pierce the plastic liner to facilitate drainage and let the sun finish the melting process. The easiest way to dispose of the plastic liner is to cut it into strips about 5 feet wide, roll them up, tie them and stack them like cordwood for the trash collector, or throw them in your car trunk if you have to dispose of them yourself. Take down the wire backstop (if it's too damaged to be re-used next season you can always give it extra service as a garden trellis for peas or cucumbers), cut away the material you used to seal the seams and gaps between the boards, then lift each board out of the ground and store it away for next season. If you exercise care in the removal and storage of the boards, they should serve you well for many seasons.